A welcomed retreat with one of t
masters of our time. An inspiratic
SR. HELEN PREJEAN, CSJ, *Ministi*

MW00462491

Pick up this book and let it guide you to reflect on the questions of your life
and the choices ahead. I was enriched by the journey into solitude (not loneliness), gratitude (not resentment), love (not fear). Through reading, journaling, and just plain savoring the message of our lives, the authors lead us
through Henri Nouwen's writings to author our own lives in vibrant ways.
The message in the end is that the world is hungry for us as we weave the community we hunger for.
SIMONE CAMPBELL, SSS

A spiritual retreat from one of the twentieth century's greatest spiritual masters.
JAMES MARTIN, SJ, *author of Learning to Pray*

This is Nouwen pure and distilled: no spiritual writer plunges us deeper into
the well of loneliness and anguish; no spiritual writer more deftly scoops us out
of our despair and self-loathing and restores us to blessedness and joy.
BRENDAN WALSH, *Editor, The Tablet, UK*

One of the great contemporary spiritual masters leads us on a transformative
journey to the sacred center. A life-changing retreat.
RICHARD ROHR, *Center for Action and Contemplation*

This extraordinary book draws on the authors' own profound knowledge of
Henri Nouwen's life and writings to invite us on a spiritual journey. Our prin-
cipal guide will be Henri, one of the great spiritual masters of the past century.
On the journey we will learn to discover—in every aspect of our lives—that
unconditional, transformative First Love that Henri knew so intimately.
ROBERTO S. GOIZUETA, *Margaret O'Brien Flatley Professor Emeritus of Catholic
Theology, Boston College*

One of Henri Nouwen's most enduring legacies is his encouragement to
create space for God in our lives. Sometimes we don't know how or where to
start. This wonderful book, written by two pastors steeped in the wisdom of
Nouwen, provides an entry point and steady companionship to follow the call
to carve out sacred time. Through profound personal stories, Scripture, as well
as key spiritual truths drawn from Nouwen's canon, you will tune into your
inner being and ponder the big questions—who you are, who God is, why suffering, how to love, and the real meaning of freedom—not with the head but
with the heart. What a gift!
GABRIELLE EARNSHAW, *Chief Archivist, The Henri Nouwen Legacy Trust,
author of Henri Nouwen and the Return of the Prodigal Son: The Making
of a Spiritual Classic*

For decades, the works of Henri Nouwen have been an enormous encouragement and thoughtful challenge to my faith, Christian practice, and spiritual theology. It would be hard to overstate Nouwen's impact on my life and engagement with God. This recourse, *On Retreat with Henri Nouwen: Engaging Life's Big Questions*, has been like spending time with an old friend—countless reminders of the ways God has used Nouwen's words in my life in the past, combined with a few new insights that have given lift to my life in Christ. I am so grateful. If you have been an avid Nouwen reader, this book will be a joyful renewal and reminder, and if Henri Nouwen's works are relatively new to you, I trust you will find a trove of thoughtfulness that will whet your appetite for more.

REV. DR. BRIAN M. WALLACE, *Executive Director, The Fuller Center for Spiritual and Missional Formation, Fuller Theological Seminary*

On Retreat with Henri Nouwen is a welcome gift during a time of worldwide uncertainty in which we have faced frightening questions about our very way of life as we've always known it. It speaks to us of Henri's incessant search for freedom beneath his many nervous apprehensions. In his personal and confessional style, he reconnects us with our deepest aspirations for love, harmony, and peace, in the heart of God.

SR. SUE MOSTELLER, CSJ, *Literary Executrix of the Henri Nouwen Legacy and Founding Member of the Henri Nouwen Legacy Trust and Henri Nouwen Society*

A great resource for individual and small group reflection, *On Retreat with Henri Nouwen* offers invaluable insights for those seeking greater clarity and meaning in their spiritual lives. Using Nouwen's own words on themes such as Identity, God, Love, Suffering, and Freedom, the authors Chris Pritchett and Marjorie J. Thompson have developed a series of reflections that offer hope and guidance for spiritual journeyers wishing a deeper understanding of what spirituality means in today's context.

C. VANESSA WHITE, DMIN, *Associate Professor of Spirituality and Ministry, Catholic Theological Union*

For those who have long journeyed with Henri Nouwen, and for those who are encountering him for the first time, *On Retreat with Henri Nouwen* offers a rich and inspiring new opportunity to come to know the essential writings of this incomparable spiritual master.

DAVID SYLVESTER, PHD, *President, University of St. Michael's College in the University of Toronto*

Spiritual discernment has become a key concept for understanding the vision of community today. We see this in many contemporary leaders, from Pope Francis to guides like Henri Nouwen. *On Retreat with Henri Nouwen* provides an essential companion for those who desire to practice discernment as an elemental component in the "art of spiritual living."

MASSIMO FAGGIOLI, *Professor of Theology and Religious Studies, Villanova University, author of Joe Biden and Catholicism in the United States (Bayard, 2021)*

INSIGHTS *from a* SPIRITUAL MASTER

On Retreat with

HENRI NOUWEN

Engaging Life's Big Questions

CHRIS PRITCHETT *and* MARJORIE J. THOMPSON

TWENTY-THIRD
PUBLICATIONS
twentythirdpublications.com

NOVALIS

TWENTY-THIRD PUBLICATIONS
One Montauk Avenue, Suite 200 • New London, CT 06320
(860) 437-3012 or (800) 321-0411 • www.twentythirdpublications.com

ISBN: 978-1-62785-614-0

Published in Canada by Novalis

Publishing Office
1 Eglinton Avenue East, Suite 800
Toronto, Ontario, Canada
M4P 3A1
www.novalis.ca

Head Office
4475 Frontenac Street
Montréal, Québec, Canada
H2H 2S2

Cataloguing in Publication is available from Library and Archives Canada.
ISBN: 978-2-89688-954-9

We acknowledge the support of the Government of Canada.
5   4   3   2   1   25   24   23   22   21

All cited works used by permission.

Cover art: ©Shutterstock.com
Printed in the U.S.A.

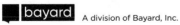 A division of Bayard, Inc.

Contents

HENRI NOUWEN (1932–1996) was one of the most innovative and influential spiritual writers of the past century. His vision of spirituality was broad and inclusive, and his compassion embraced all of humankind. Nouwen was born in the Netherlands, the eldest of four children in a devout Roman Catholic family. He was attracted to the religious life as a child and ordained to the priesthood in 1957 at a time when the Catholic Church was moving toward the historic reforms of the Second Vatican Council. These more inclusive attitudes influenced Henri deeply. After studying psychology in Holland, he traveled to the U.S. where he enrolled at the Menninger Institute in Topeka, Kansas, the birthplace of pastoral psychology. He taught in this field at Notre Dame and later taught pastoral ministry and spirituality both at Yale and Harvard Divinity Schools. These years were fruitful in published writings as well. Living among the poor in Peru, along with an introduction to the L'Arche community in Trosly-Breuil, France, planted the seeds of Henri's move from academia to the L'Arche Daybreak community outside Toronto in 1986. He experienced the invitation to be their pastor as a genuine call of God and spent his final ten years of life there with the community he called home. On a trip back to Holland in 1996, Henri succumbed to a heart attack. By the time of his death, he had written almost forty books on spirituality and the spiritual life that have sold millions of copies and been translated into more than thirty languages. He remains one of the most beloved spiritual writers of the twentieth century. The passages quoted in this book are taken from certain of his published works, all of which are available at www.henrinouwen.org.

INTRODUCTION

"He has a literal prayer closet," Henri's assistant John assured me. "You have seen it?" I queried. "Yes, just a tiny closet with a small table set up as an altar." John described the cloth, icon, chalice, and prayer book. He continued, "Henri talks about his struggles with prayer, but Henri prays every day in that little closet." As Nouwen's teaching, research, and editorial assistant for five years at Yale Divinity School, John knew his mentor well. My own glimpses into the personal practice of this spiritual giant were expanded when, a few years later, John became my spouse and I entered the friendship he and Henri shared.

Henri Nouwen was truly a spiritual master of the twentieth century. His legacy secures him a place of high honor in the Christian lineage of formative teachers, writers, and spiritual guides. Nouwen was a man of many words—author of more than forty books, widely sought speaker, and mentor through letters to literally thousands of people around the globe. Yet his life spoke as clearly as his words. It was a life marked by intense struggle alongside intense joy—the central paradox of his own journey. By listening prayerfully to his own struggles and joys, Henri was able to open up his spiritual discoveries and insights to others in a remarkably accessible way. His gift to the world remains the uniquely woven depth and simplicity of his teaching on the Christian spiritual life.

This book is a contribution to the commemoration of the twenty-fifth anniversary of Henri Nouwen's death. It is intended to acquaint the reader more closely with wisdom that draws us into the healing gift of Christ's love for all humanity. Each chapter of this book reflects ideas and themes related to the art of living an authentically Christian life, deeply central to Nouwen's work. Just as he himself wrestled with and grew through engaging these themes in his life, Nouwen's writing on these topics invites us into our own deeper growth in receiving and giving God's faithful love.

"The Art of Living" can only be understood as the art of spiritual living in Henri's lexicon. He was not interested in a life animated or enamored by the world's values. Indeed, those who knew Henri soon discovered that he was only tenuously rooted in this physical world. His interest in food was largely a matter of ingesting adequate calories. At table with friends or colleagues, he savored physical food far less than conversation. John recalled regular lunches at Henri's apartment, where he was served Campbell's Golden Mushroom Soup, to which Henri had proudly added a dash of wine. Clothing was not of particular concern to Henri either. His basic outfit was predictable. Once, he joined a camping trip, attired in the same dark slacks, white shirt, and loafers he would have worn to the lecture hall. Henri's mind and heart were fixed on God's presence in this world. His ministry was an invitation to enter spiritual communion with Christ through contemplative prayer, and from this centered heart to offer compassionate service to the world God so loves. Henri's invitation to us mirrors his own call to live fearlessly in the Spirit while alive in this world.

Nouwen occasionally led retreats, and retreats were certainly part of his own formation as a priest. When I audited classes with Henri as a research fellow at Yale, he urged me to make a forty-day Ignatian retreat at the same Jesuit center in Ontario where he had made his retreat years earlier. Henri knew the importance of giving ourselves stretches of time to rest in God's presence and simply listen. I suspect Nouwen's strong emphasis on solitude, prayer, and written reflection stems from his own experience with extended retreat. A few years before I first met Henri, he had been granted the highly unusual privilege of being received as a "temporary monk" at the Trappist Abbey of Genesee in upstate New York. For Henri, this represented a seven-month step away from his class schedule and speaking circuit in order, as he put it, to face his own compulsions and illusions. In his introduction to the diary he kept during this first stay at Genesee, he asks, "Is there a still point where my life is anchored and from which I can reach out with hope and courage and confidence?"[1] Perhaps Henri's words resonate as a motivating question in our own desire for spiritual retreat.

I invite you to allow this book to serve as a guide into your own personal retreat. Each time you read a portion of these pages, let yourself step into a space apart from your ordinary activities and preoccupations. Whether you are indoors or in the natural world, allow this to be a time for prayerful reflection and meditation—as if the place in which you read and journal were your private sanctuary. There is no particular timeframe for this retreat. You can take it as deliberately as you like. Nouwen's wisdom will serve in some ways as your guide. Yet Henri would want you to remember that by choosing to open more intentionally to God, the Holy Spirit becomes your true spiritual director.

The chapters of this book represent a natural sequence in our spiritual life. It begins with questions about our identity: Who am I? As our seeking leads us to discover our true identity in God, the question becomes: Who is God? Our images and understandings of God, explored and expanded, lead us to the very core of divine being—Love. Love seems like the happy answer to all our heartfelt desires; yet we find ourselves foundering on the rocks of suffering—personal and collective human pain. How can we understand the relationship between God's love and our suffering? The challenges of suffering lead us finally to consider the relationship between life and death. These themes form the arc of the book and supply its chapter titles.

While living at the Genesee, Henri met regularly with his spiritual director, Abbot John Eudes Bamberger. One day Henri asked, "When I pray, to whom do I pray?" The abbot replied, "This is the real question….You will discover that it involves every part of yourself because the question, Who is the Lord to whom I pray? leads directly to the question, Who am I who wants to pray to the Lord?…This leads you to the center of meditation."[2] Father John Eudes might well have quoted one of the lifelong prayers of St. Francis of Assisi: "Who am I, O God; and Who art Thou?" While simple, these questions cannot be answered simplistically. In the course of faith maturation we find partial answers, not definitive ones. Rather, such questions carry us straight to the heart of an inexhaustible Mystery. This makes them good questions for the start of your retreat.

Each chapter concludes with reflection questions. Choose those that speak to your life and draw your heart to reflection. One question may raise for you a related question not suggested, which you sense is more important to consider. Follow the inner prompting of the Spirit.

Along with questions, you will find a few "action" suggestions to select from. They are designed to help you go deeper: perhaps using imagination to open up a Scripture text or a sketched image to explore the theme more fully; maybe they will inspire a new commitment in your spiritual practice or reaching out to another person. Such active exercises serve to integrate our human faculties, stimulating change in habitual ways of thinking, feeling, speaking, and acting. Prayerful reflection and action thus help us enter more fully into the mind of Christ (see Philippians 2:5).

To gain the greatest benefit from retreat it is helpful to keep a journal. For Henri Nouwen, writing was a spiritual practice. He wrote so much that he was sometimes accused of never having an unpublished thought. But as my husband came to see, with gentler clarity, "Henri processed his life through his pen." With time, Henri learned this about himself: "I become more and more aware that for me writing is a very powerful way of concentrating and of clarifying for myself many thoughts and feelings. Once I put my pen on paper and write for an hour or two, a real sense of peace and harmony comes for me."[3] Henri came to see his life more clearly and calmly through writing.

The benefits of journaling in tandem with prayerful meditation are many. The first relates to what Henri articulated: the very process of writing down thoughts tends to clarify them. Ideas swimming around our heads can get confused and jumbled. Writing helps sort them out, making them concrete and specific. As we make better sense of our thoughts, we find greater meaning in them. The second benefit is that recording our experience allows us to track insights over time. Writing helps us remember what might otherwise be a fleeting memory or impression. This in turn allows us to see how our insights grow, change, and connect with other learnings over time. Keeping a journal can help us recognize themes that recur in our spiritual journey, adding deeper dimensions with new life experiences. A journal helps us record and track spiritual growth.

Of course, not everyone is drawn to keeping a journal. Some of us even feel a strong resistance to doing so. We may fear that prying eyes will discover our secret thoughts, doubts, and struggles. Perhaps we have tried and found journaling too time-consuming. Maybe we lack confidence in writing skills. Here are a few suggestions for relieving these reservations and unburdening our practice of journaling:

1. Be clear that a spiritual journal is for your eyes only. It is intended as a place to freely explore what's in your mind and heart—ideas, feelings, inspirations, wonderings, connections—in the presence of a divine love that fosters freedom. You are at liberty to share whatever you wish with whomever you choose, or to keep your journal entirely confidential. To ensure confidentiality, find a secure place to keep your journal or, if using an electronic device, give it strong password protection.

2. This journal is purely for your growth, and since no one will be grading it you can write any way that suits you. Good grammar, spelling, and complete sentences are not required. It doesn't have to be beautiful, poetic, or profound. Place no expectations on what a journal "should be" and simply allow your words to emerge naturally. Jot notes in sentence fragments; add doodles or illustrations. We can be playful while taking the reflection process seriously.

If you choose to use a hard-copy journal, dedicate one specifically to this retreat—perhaps a spiral-bound notebook or a blank-page book. Make sure you have a pen at hand before you start reading. You may want to jot questions or insights that arise as you go. A journal allows you to collect your thoughts all in one place.

This retreat combines three elements: the book, your journal, and the physical space in which you read and reflect. These elements are held within the larger context of God's guiding presence. You will want to invite the Holy Spirit into your retreat each time you sit down to read as well as offer gratitude for gifts received at the end of each period of reflection.

The retreat structure is up to you. You might assign yourself a specific time each day or week, such as twenty minutes daily, or an hour on the weekend. You might prefer to commit to one section of a chapter each evening before bed. Do take account of your energy patterns. If you are too sleepy before bed, you won't benefit much from reflection at this hour.

As with any retreat, do your best to secure quiet space uninterrupted by family members, housemates, calls, or electronic pings. Let those with whom you live know when you plan to be unavailable. Turn off cell phones and other distracting devices for the period in which you are choosing to be available to God and your deeper self. Silence is never absolute in our lives, but we can usually achieve a helpful measure of quiet when we are intentional about protecting temporary solitude.

All that remains is to invite into our heart's sanctuary the very God of heaven and earth, the Lord who promises to abide with us always, the Spirit who guides us into the fullness of life, healing, and peace. Henri invites us now to listen more deeply, trust more fully, and find our greatest joy in more intimate communion with our living Source.

CHAPTER ONE

Identity

Finding Myself in God

"Those two are brothers," Joseph said with a thick Kenyan accent. From his driver's seat, he pointed to two stunning cheetahs calmly walking through the valley of the Masai Mara. It was sunset. My twelve-year-old daughter and I were on a safari at the tail end of a visit to Nairobi. Joseph was our guide. He camped with us for three days and led us through the breathtaking wilderness. Joseph knew where to go and when. He knew how many leopards lived there and where certain animals fed. He was well aware of off-trail locations where lions were sure to be sleeping. He knew when to leave a herd of elephants because that particular "Mama" would charge the van. Without a skillful guide, we would have been lost or even dead.

In many ways, the spiritual life is not unlike a safari in the wilderness. There is such breathtaking beauty, a world of wonder, and it helps to have a skillful guide who knows the terrain and can show others where to find what they came to discover. Father Henri J.M. Nouwen continues to be among the most beloved of such spiritual guides.

This chapter addresses the concept of identity and explores the topic of our belovedness—vital components of Nouwen's writing. Henri writes: "When we honestly ask ourselves which persons in our lives mean the most to us, we often find that it is those who, instead of giving much advice, solutions, or cures, have chosen rather to share our pain and touch our wounds with a gentle and tender hand."[4] Henri Nouwen is one who can guide us through the wilderness of some of the deepest questions we ask, one of them being, "Who am I?"

BELOVEDNESS

One of the most important questions we can ask ourselves is, "Who am I?" Along with determining our purpose and place in this world, finding our true identity is something sociologists suggest every young person must discover in order to flourish in adulthood. Historically, young people have tried to find identity primarily through participating in rites of passage, like confirmation or a bar/bat mitzvah. Today, we often leave it to young people to determine their identity for themselves through the choices they make in life. We say, "If you choose to work hard and get into medical school, you can become a doctor, and that will be who you are." This puts tremendous pressure on them to create their own identity.

In his many writings, Henri Nouwen addressed the concept of identity, and the question of identity, by reframing our approach. For Nouwen, the answer to "Who am I?" comes not from what we do but from who God created us to be. In the first chapter of Genesis, we are reminded that humankind is made in God's image, the heart of which is love. We are God's beloved children, and it is this belovedness that motivates and marks us. As Henri proclaims, "Being the beloved expresses the core truth of our existence."[5] We belong to God and always will. We may well know this in our minds, yet social pressures tempt us to display an image of ourselves that we hope will be more acceptable. We have a hunger to be accepted by people, even if that means presenting an image that is a fabrication of our true identity.

This behavior was on display for all to see in the 2019 college admissions scandal in the United States, the largest scandal in the history of college admissions in North America. Hundreds among the wealthiest elites in the United States, from CEOs to Hollywood stars, were caught in a web of bribery and fraud, having paid millions to get their overly privileged yet apparently underperforming kids into some of the most elite universities in the nation. It seems that the motivating factor for these parents was the social applause of having a child at USC instead of Cal State Long Beach, or Stanford instead of San Francisco State. This scandal revealed the desire to make the public believe that these kids got in on their own merits. Here is the message I believe these parents have sent their kids: *"You matter to the degree that you perform, or to the degree that you make me look good, or to the degree that you are successful, popular, and good looking."* The truth is, this is the message many young people grow up hearing today. From our earliest years, we are praised for getting good grades and punished for low achievement.

According to Nouwen, we slowly grow to believe the lies that *I am what I do, I am what others say about me,* and *I am what I possess.* That is why Henri's message of our truer and deeper identity as beloved children of God is so important. It is an identity not tossed about with the waves of success, failure, joy, and sorrow in life. "The great secret of the spiritual life," Nouwen wrote, "the life of the Beloved Sons and Daughters of God, is that everything we live, be it gladness or sadness, joy or pain, health or illness, can all be part of the journey toward the full realization of our humanity."[6]

Nouwen believed that we can claim our true identity as we grow to see ourselves in two moments in the life of Jesus: his baptism and his final Passover meal. Let's take each moment in turn.

In the baptism of Jesus, we see what many scholars have considered the first reference to the Trinity in the New Testament. When John the Baptist had submerged Jesus into the River Jordan, "just as he came up from the water, suddenly the heavens were opened to him and he saw the Spirit of God descending like a dove and alighting on him. And a voice from heaven said, 'This is my Son, the Beloved, with whom I am well pleased'" (Matthew 3:16–17).

But why did Jesus choose to be baptized when he did not need to repent? Most theologians agree that it was in order to identify with us and our need to be reconciled with God. It is incredibly significant that Jesus does not receive the Father's designation as the beloved until he identifies with us by being baptized in the Jordan. He does not receive the title at his birth or during his early life. No, it comes when he enters into our desperation in an identification that is so total and complete that you can hear God saying this to you as well. This is the most surprising gift—that God says to you as well as to Jesus: *"You are my priceless child; I am deeply pleased with you."* That is who you are.

The church teaches that in our baptism we are given the gift of the Holy Spirit, who binds us into the Son's relationship with the Father. It is in baptism that we are welcomed into the covenant community and entrusted to the church for the spiritual guidance that nurtures us to claim our true created identity as the beloved of God.

The second moment in Jesus' life we are meant to see ourselves in is "the Last Supper," which the church celebrates sacramentally in the Eucharist. Nouwen believed that every time we participate in the Eucharist, we are to remember how greatly pleased God is with us. When Jesus celebrated his last Passover meal with his disciples in the upper room (also known as "the Lord's Supper"), he used four actions or movements. Each movement is represented with a word that helps us to claim our truest and deepest identity as the beloved: *Take, Bless, Break, Give.*

1. Replacing the word "take" with "choose," Nouwen says that, in the same way Jesus "chose" the bread, he has also chosen you from before the foundation of the world. To be chosen by God is the greatest gift and deepest experience of being human. God's choosing is not competitive or based on your merit but is generous, based on God's goodness and love.

2. After Jesus took the bread, he "blessed it." To be blessed by God is to be given God's favor. It is a love and favor so deep, so wide, and so complete that it covers over all the failures of those whom we needed to bless us but did not. Nouwen writes, "A blessing goes beyond the distinction between admiration or condemnation...between good deeds or evil deeds. A blessing touches the original goodness of the other and calls forth his or her Belovedness."[7]

3. Though we have been given God's blessing, we are also wounded people in a broken world. We are all recipients, participants, and inheritors of this fractured cosmos. After "giving thanks," or "blessing" the bread, Jesus "broke" it. Nouwen helps us to see that this breaking of the bread is an image of the brokenness of each of our lives. Henri suggests that we can find freedom and new life

if we have the courage to embrace our brokenness. In doing this, we may press through our brokenness and arrive on the other side. But, he says, we must always remember to "put it under the blessing."[8] We are to embrace our brokenness, but not as our core identity. Because the blessing comes before the brokenness, we are to remember that our identity as "the beloved" (blessing) is deeper and truer than our experience of suffering (brokenness).

4. Finally, Jesus "gave" the bread to the disciples and invited them to eat it and remember him. Just as Jesus was "chosen" and "blessed" in his baptism (as are we in ours), Jesus' heart was broken on the cross (as are we in life). Jesus was then able to be "given" to the world for its salvation. In the same way, Nouwen says that we are "chosen," "blessed," and "broken," in order that we may be "given" or sent by God for the sake of others. If we live our lives either avoiding our brokenness or claiming it as our deepest identity, thereby forgetting that we are first chosen and blessed by God, our lives will be tossed about by the waves of insecurity, anger, and discontent.

Instead, Nouwen invites us to hear the voice of God our heavenly Father, who is so pleased with us. He is pleased not because of what we have done but because of who we most deeply are—creatures on whom God has bestowed the divine image. Before the fall of humankind lies the deeper truth that we are loved for all eternity. You are the beloved not because you finally figured out how to choose the right way. You are the beloved of God because you have always belonged to God. In the baptism of Jesus, God has found you again. In every Eucharist, God reminds you again. Nouwen invites us to prayerfully attend to God's personal words of love and favor, saying, "Every time you listen with great attentiveness to the voice that calls you the Beloved, you will discover within yourself a desire to hear that voice longer and more deeply."[9]

Henri Nouwen believed that we come to discover our true selves best in solitude: "In solitude we discover that our life is not a possession to be defended but a gift to be shared."[10] Tamp down the noise in your life so that you can hear the still, small voice calling us the Beloved. Take some time this week to be in solitude with God. Let the Spirit be present with you in your reflections and prayers. It will serve as a deep well of living water from which you can draw in times of success to remain humble and in times of distress to remain hopeful.

※　　※　　※

BELONGING

As long as we belong to this world, we will remain subject to its competitive ways and expect to be rewarded for all the good we do. But when we belong to God, who loves us without conditions, we can live as he does.[11]

In the spring of my first year as an undergraduate student in college, I tried out for the men's soccer team as a "walk-on." I had played soccer with some success all through high school. Many of the players on the college team were my friends, and I played soccer with them for fun on a regular basis. After several weeks of tryouts, the assistant coach gave me notice that I was cut from the team. I was devastated. I had always belonged on the soccer field with my teammates. Suddenly, I felt not only rejection but a sense of disorientation. Something that was supposed to be part of my life no longer was. Every time I saw the players, I was confronted with the reality that I did not belong to the team. Every time they had a home game, I would hide my pain with laughter and cheer as I rooted for the team from the bleachers. When we do not have a deep sense of belonging, we experience feelings of rejection more acutely. When we experience rejection, we quickly forget that we are loved and can easily say to ourselves, "I am not good enough." Or, "I am not worthy." Our feelings of being rejected by others become the justification by which we then reject ourselves. "It must be true," we might think, or "I do not belong here."

But a "deep sense" of belonging is not tossed to and fro by the experiences and feelings of acceptance or rejection in everyday life. Our temporary experiences of rejection are never the last word. When we do experience rejection, a deep sense of belonging reminds us of the profound truth that in fact we belong to one another, to ourselves, and to the world, precisely because we belong to God from everlasting to everlasting. A deep sense of belonging is rooted in the knowledge of our eternal belovedness. No group, no soccer team, no community or nation can take that truth away. We belong to God and in God's family for all eternity. When we know this to be true— not just with our intellect but in our heart—we are given the gifts of patience, resilience, and faith.

There was a time in Henri Nouwen's life when he experienced great anguish. This season of inner turmoil took place from December 1987 to June 1988, after he had left his prestigious position as a professor at Harvard Divinity School in order to serve alongside persons with disabilities at the L'Arche Daybreak Community in Toronto. He referred to this as the most difficult season in his life. Reflecting on his anguish, Nouwen wrote: "I had come face to face with my own nothingness. It was as if all that had given my life meaning was pulled away and I could see nothing in front of me but a bottomless abyss."[12] During these months, Henri wrote an intimate and intense "secret" journal that, by the encouragement of his friends, was later published as *The Inner Voice of Love*. In this book, Nouwen wrote sixty-three imperatives. We will look at three of these commands. Each of them teaches us something valuable about the "deep sense" of belonging, what it involves, and how it is formed in our lives.

The first imperative: *Accept Your Identity as a Child of God.* Henri wrote to himself: "Your true identity is as a child of God. This is the identity you have to accept. Once you have claimed it and settled in it, you can live in a world that gives you much joy as well as pain."[13]

According to Nouwen, our lives here on earth are momentary experiences where God gives us the opportunity not only to accept divine love for us but to say, "I love you," back. To be clear, Nouwen did not imagine that once we have claimed our deepest identity as children of God we no longer need the love and acceptance of other human beings. Not at all. We do, in fact, need the imperfect love of family and friends to remind us that we are perfectly loved only by a Love surpassing any human love. Nouwen went on to write: "You need spiritual guidance; you need people who can keep you anchored in your true identity."[14]

The second imperative: *Claim Your Unique Presence in Your Community.* "Your unique presence in your community is the way God wants you to be present to others. Different people have different ways of being present. You have to know and claim your way.... That will help you decide what to do and what to let go of, what to say and what to remain silent about, when to go out and when to stay home, who to be with and who to avoid."[15] Henri learned this imperative the hard way. He loved being with people but had so much love to give that he often exhausted himself in caregiving and ended his day feeling lonely and depressed.

On the one hand, Nouwen loved people and wanted to share Jesus' love with them; on the other hand, he recognized that he often acted from his own need to be loved *by* others, a need that sometimes drove people away from him. Then he would find himself feeling rejected and empty, as though his well had run dry. Henri discovered that only God can give the kind of sustainable and resilient love for which he was looking. Only God could offer him the "living water" (John 7:37–38) of complete belonging.

Nouwen writes, "Your way of being present to your community may require times of absence, prayer, writing, or solitude. These too are times for your community. They allow you to be deeply present to your people and speak words that come from God in you."[16] Through his practice of solitude and prayer, Henri learned how to love well and find joy in being with God. He learned how to let go of expecting the community to meet all his needs and discovered the deep rest of belonging to God's love.

The third imperative: *Always Come Back to the Solid Place*. "You must believe in the yes that comes back when you ask, 'Do you love me?' You must *choose* this yes even when you do not experience it."[17]

The key word here is *choose*. Faith is always a choice. Love is always a choice. We are constantly receiving messages that tell us we do not belong. We are told that we belong only *if* we work hard or dress a certain way or make a certain amount of money. At the beginning and the end of each day, we must choose to believe that we belong to God.

This truth will take deep root in our souls over time and become the spiritual anchor of our lives.

IMAGO DEI

> When I write to you that, as the Beloved, we are God's chosen ones, I mean that we have been seen by God from all eternity and seen as unique, special, precious beings.[18]

I repeat this quote because it is so central to an authentic spiritual life yet so difficult to truly live out. How do I claim my identity as a child of God? At some level I've known it to be true since I was a child. This is what the church taught me over and over again. But to realize it fully, to know it to be true at a deep, heartfelt level has been, and will continue to be, the journey of my life. It sounds so simple—*your true identity is as a child of God*—but let's unpack what it means. In the very beginning of the Bible, the Hebrew writers tell of the creation of the entire cosmos using poetic verse to convey the beauty and creative majesty of the Creator. The amazing truth is, of all God's loving creatures, only humankind was created in God's "image and likeness" (Genesis 1:26–27). God's character, nature, and wisdom are uniquely given to humankind, for the purpose of exercising good stewardship over the natural world. The Latin phrase for "image of God" is *imago Dei*. It expresses a very positive "theological anthropology," which means a high view of human life and purpose in the cosmos. To be made in the *imago Dei* means that before there was an "original sin," there was an "original blessing."

Have you ever wondered why many people who do not profess

faith in God can live such morally admirable lives? Or why many who do profess faith in God often seem morally bankrupt or confused? First, all humankind is created in the divine image, not just Christians, so we often see little moral difference between people who profess faith and those who do not. To be created in God's image means that within every human being lives the goodness, kindness, love, wisdom, and benevolence of God.

Yet just as all people are created in the image of God, so too are all people sinners. Therefore, it is sometimes difficult to recognize the difference between a person who professes faith in God and one who does not. The difference lies in whether the person of faith makes the effort, by God's grace, to pursue the spiritual journey of transformation. This journey is first and foremost about a transformed sense of identity. We are seeking to recover our deepest identity, which has been profaned both by our own choices and by the choices of others. The truth of our identity is that we are children of God who bear the *imago Dei* in our created being. But as the years go by, we bear the wounds that others give us. We also, sadly, wound ourselves and others in response. We believe the myriad lies that society tells us about who we are. We live from our false selves, our egos, which generally feel fearful, defensive, and punitive.

In his book *The Way of the Heart*, Henri reflects on the importance of grasping the distinction between our true and false selves. He writes:

> The secular or false self is the self which is fabricated, as Thomas Merton says, by social compulsions. "Compulsive" is indeed the best adjective for the false self. It points to the need for ongoing and increasing affirma-

tion. Who am I? I am the one is who is liked, praised, admired, disliked, hated or despised....If being busy is a good thing, then I must be busy. If having money is a sign of real freedom, then I must claim my money. If knowing many people proves my importance, I will have to make the necessary contacts. The compulsion manifests itself in the lurking fear of failing and the steady urge to prevent this by gathering more of the same—more work, more money, more friends.

These very compulsions are at the basis of the two main enemies of the spiritual life: anger and greed. They are the inner side of a secular life, the sour fruits of our worldly dependencies.[19]

❃   ❃   ❃

At the core of who we are is the reality that we are created out of the overflowing generative love of a Trinitarian God who knows no other way of being than to love. To be made in the image of such a God is to know that we are made for intimacy. We first see this in the creation narratives when God creates Adam and Eve for one another. They are also created to be in loving relationship together with God. This means that we all are made for joy and peace and for a world in original harmony without competition or conflict. Yet it is the fallen world in which we find ourselves, as recounted in Genesis 3. So to discover a deep sense of *imago Dei* within us means learning to see that the identities we construct through our own actions are very limited identities. Being athletic, beautiful, successful, influential, or famous is merely part of a world that is passing. Striving for these things can help us learn about ourselves to some extent. They are not wholly without meaning, but they are temporary. Our deepest identity in God is given to us—there is nothing we could do to bolster or to minimize it.

A friend of mine by the name of Steve grew up in Southern California and entered into adulthood as a strapping young man. Standing six feet four inches tall, he was lean and strong with sun-browned skin and thick brown hair. Steve was an incredible surfer and a top student. After college, Steve married a beautiful young woman. Together, they had four boys. He was as a successful real estate agent and a wonderful husband and father. But on New Year's Eve 2015, on his way home from a mountain bike ride, Steve was hit by a drunk driver and suffered a major brain injury. He was completely paralyzed and placed in a coma. Today, Steve lives fully paralyzed and unable to communicate with the outside world. His injury took away every one of the identities he had constructed for himself—popular, good-looking, athlete, successful, beautiful family man. In a moment's time they were all taken away by the deplorable decision of an irresponsible partier. But his truest identity as a beloved child of God remains unscathed.

Life often takes unexpected turns. We lose what we had gained, or we discover that the things we thought would bring satisfaction have left us wanting.

It's as though we have two identities struggling to prevail inside us. Thomas Merton called them our "true self" and our "false self." The apostle Paul called them "the old self" and "the new self," or the way of "the flesh" and the way of "the Spirit." The "true self" is the identity that lives within us—a "home" or "dwelling place" that exists beyond time and space, in mystery, love, goodness, and truth. In this house we are truly known and perfectly loved, from everlasting to everlasting, at peace and safe from all distress. To know that we are made in the *imago Dei* is to know where we belong, in which house we are meant to dwell. This is the identity we are all seeking to recover.

But it is not easy to recover this identity or to dwell in this "house of the Lord." We are taught by the world to put our trust in the houses we construct for ourselves. Therefore, we put our trust in what we think will protect us in this life. But then loss or tragedy befalls us, our dreams go unrealized, and once again we ask ourselves, "Who am I now?" What we truly need is to dwell in a place that can endure these storms, even the storm of death.

Nouwen offers us guidance by helping us see that to dwell in our eternal home involves letting go. He writes:

> I know that true joy comes from letting God love me the way God wants, whether it is through illness or health, failure or success, poverty or wealth, rejection or praise. It is hard for me to say, "I shall gratefully accept everything, Lord, that pleases you. Let your will be done." But I know that when I truly believe my Father is pure love, it will become increasingly possible to say these words from the heart.
>
> Charles de Foucauld once wrote a prayer of abandonment that expresses beautifully the spiritual attitude I wish I had....
>
> *Father, I abandon myself into your hands;*
> *do with me what you will.*
> *Whatever you may do, I thank you;*
> *I am ready for all, I accept all.*

Let only your will be done in me,
and in all your creatures.

I wish no more than this,
O Lord.
Into your hands I commend my soul;
I offer it to you with all the love of my heart,
for I love you, Lord,
and so need to give myself,
to surrender myself into your hands
without reserve
and with boundless confidence.
For you are my Father.

It seems good to pray this prayer often. These are the words of a holy man, and they show the way I must go. I realize that I can never make this prayer come true by my own efforts. But the spirit of Jesus given to me can help me pray it and grow to its fulfillment. I know that my inner peace depends on my willingness to make this prayer my own.[20]

FALSE NARRATIVES

Personally, as my struggle reveals, I don't often "feel" like a beloved child of God. But I know that that is my most primal identity and I know that I must choose it above and beyond my hesitations.[21]

One of the great challenges nearly everyone has to face is learning to come to terms with the negative and false messages we have received through the years. Without serious and intentional reflection, we hold these messages in various corners of our hearts without realizing it. Just as a buildup of toxins in the body can lead to physical illness, a buildup of negative messages about who we are can often lead to unhealthy and regrettable social behavior, if not mental illness. These toxic messages rob us of our joy and satisfaction. The opening pages of Genesis remind us of the theological truth that we are made in God's image, yet they also tell of the very first lie we chose to believe. It was a lie about our identity. The serpent led Adam and Eve to believe that they could experience more of life than they were promised by their Creator:

> Now the serpent was more crafty than any of the wild animals the Lord God had made. He said to the woman, "Did God really say, 'You must not eat from any tree in the garden'?" The woman said to the serpent, "We may eat fruit from the trees in the garden, but God did say, 'You must not eat fruit from the tree that is in the middle of the garden, and you must not touch it, or you will die.'" "You will not surely die," the serpent said to the woman. "For God knows that when you eat of it your eyes will be opened, and you will be like God, knowing good and evil." GENESIS 3:1–5

The underlying message from the serpent to the humans was, "Who you are right now is not good enough. Your life should be better. You can improve who you are." Ever since, we have been striving to prove ourselves. We take matters into our own hands.

There are five primary negative identity messages that we receive in various ways throughout life. They are subtle and seep into our self-understanding. This has always been the human experience. Our true self, as pointed out, is the one given us at creation and affirmed in Genesis 1:26–27. Our false self is the accumulation of all the lies we have believed about our identities. The spiritual journey is largely about shedding the false identities in order for the true identity to emerge restored and operative in one's life. Henri Nouwen wrote extensively on each of these "false identities."

The first is *I am what I have*. It is very easy to attach our sense of self-worth to our possessions, and even more to our closest relationships. Our nearest relationships quite naturally shape our sense of identity and worth, in positive and negative ways. But what happens when possessions are lost or relationships taken away? Is our sense of identity deeply shaken? Do we sink into despair and confusion? These "I haves" are meant to be understood as blessings to be offered to the world in love. Each relationship and possession ultimately belongs to God. What we truly "have" are our created, beloved identities given to us by God, along with a promise of eternal life in loving fellowship with God and creation. In his foundational book on the subject, Henri Nouwen writes:

> You have to keep unmasking the world about you for
> what it is: manipulative, controlling, power-hungry and,
> in the long run, destructive. The world tells you many
> lies about who you are, and you simply have to be real-
> istic enough to remind yourself of this. Every time you
> feel hurt, offended or rejected, you have to dare to say to
> yourself: "These feelings, strong as they may be, are not

telling me the truth about myself. The truth, even though I cannot feel it right now, is that I am the chosen child of God, precious in God's eyes, called the Beloved from all eternity, and held safe in an everlasting embrace."[22]

The second false narrative is *I am what I do*. Our culture teaches us to identify who we are with what we do. Moreover, it's not so easy to say *I am* not *what I do*, because who we are and who we grow into can be deeply shaped by our work. Our work is the means by which we give ourselves to the world. Christians believe that every person has a vocation, a called purpose to serve the world in a particular way in the name of Jesus. But, like our possessions, the talents and skills we employ are gifts given to us by God. If we lose our job, we may ask, "Who am I now?" The deeper answer never changes because it is rooted beyond our abilities and particular roles.

A third false narrative that commonly creeps into our subconscious is *I am what others say about me*. This narrative often begins in the childhood years and can easily affect the way we live through our adult years as well. The late former pastor of University Presbyterian Church in Seattle, Bruce Larson, observed that "some of us go through life listening to voices from the cellar, while others hear the voice from the balcony. From below us are the cellar influences of harsh words that were said early in our childhood: 'You're not good enough. You're not pretty. You're not very smart.' Although we have tried to rise above those judgments and have built very successful lives, we can still hear the voices from the past. They seep up through the floorboards and haunt us our whole life."[23]

The challenge, Larson continues, is "to listen to the voice from the balcony. It is the only one that can drown out the nonsense from the cellar. It is the voice of God, the heavenly Father, who is so pleased with you. He is pleased not because of what you have done but because of what Jesus has done. He found you in the wilderness and brought you home."[24]

The fourth false narrative is *I am nothing more than my worst moment*, and the fifth is its mirror, *I am nothing less than my best moment*. Each of these stories burdens us with a false sense of pressure while appealing to something heroic in us. The fourth tells us we can never rise above the shame of the weakest, most broken parts of our life. It leaves no room for growth, change, or redemption, trapping us in a deflated sense of self. The second tells us we can never be wrong, never acknowledge weakness or failure. It traps us in an artificially inflated sense of self. Neither narrative is realistic because neither allows us to be a fully human mix of shadow and light. Each is a powerful and destructive story line. Believing either one only leads to despair.

Henri Nouwen was more focused on the fourth false narrative than the fifth, reflecting his own deep struggle. In relation to it, his words below are exceptionally empowering:

> Strong emotions, self-rejection, and even self-hatred jus-
> tifiably toss you about, but you are free to respond as you
> will. You are *not* what others, or even you, think about
> yourself. You are *not* what you do. You are *not* what you
> have. You are a full member of the human family, having
> been known before you were conceived and molded in
> your mother's womb. In times when you feel bad about
> yourself, try to choose to remain true to the truth of who
> you really are. Look in the mirror each day and claim

your true identity. Act ahead of your feelings and trust that one day your feelings will match your convictions. Choose now and continue to choose this incredible truth. As a spiritual practice claim and reclaim your primal identity as beloved daughter or son of a personal Creator.[25]

ACCEPTANCE

Self-rejection is the greatest enemy of the spiritual life because it contradicts the sacred voice that calls us the "Beloved." Being the Beloved expresses the core truth of our existence.[26]

For the past twenty-five years, since my early teens, I have battled chronic depression. The potential causes of this condition are beside the point, but the illness has been very real for me most of my life. Part of this condition is linked to a struggle with self-rejection. Only in recent years, and through a great deal of inner work with a spiritual director, have I been able to recognize and address my efforts to overcompensate for my insecurities by striving to impress and please others. I thought that if people would accept me, especially people I admired (even those I would never meet), then maybe I would be able to accept myself. I had become so critical of myself that I had little capacity to receive even constructive criticism. The best way, I thought, to avoid criticism was to give no one a reason to criticize me. When I set out into adulthood with a vocation in parish ministry, I had a growing family. I quickly found myself navigating competing demands on my time and attention. I was faced with varying opinions of my leadership style. I put so much pressure on myself to win people over but had never won over myself. Even more, while I quickly realized that I would never be able to please everyone, I would not give up trying until I first began to deal with my self-rejection.

This is not a problem unique to me. Henri Nouwen articulated his similar struggle in this way:

> Over the years, I have come to realize that the greatest trap in our life is not success, popularity or power, but self-rejection. Success, popularity and power can, indeed, present a great temptation, but their seductive quality often comes from the way they are part of the much larger temptation to self-rejection. When we have come to believe in the voices that call us worthless and unlovable, then success, popularity and power are easily perceived as attractive solutions.
>
> The real trap, however, is self-rejection....As soon as someone accuses me or criticizes me, as soon as I am rejected, left alone or abandoned, I find myself thinking: "Well, that proves once again that I am a nobody."...My dark side says: I am no good....I deserve to be pushed aside, forgotten, rejected and abandoned.[27]

Henri has been one of the spiritual guides who has helped me in this particular journey. When I first read his book *Life of the Beloved* in my mid-twenties, I began thinking of my personal story in a new way. Prior to this, I would say and believe, "God loves me," but in the back of my mind I had an "anyway" attached: "God loves me, anyway." While this is absolutely a true statement about God's capacity to love me unconditionally, it was an incomplete statement about my inherent lovability. God loves me anyway, not only because God is love, but also, more important, because from that love God created me. And God creates only beauty, life, and goodness. That's not to say that I have free rein to sin. Not at all. But Henri taught me to trust the inherent goodness or blessing (*imago Dei*) that is my deeper identity, deeper than my brokenness or bad behavior.

It's hard to hold these two aspects of our human nature together. While many theologians and Christian leaders focus almost exclusively on our sinful nature, others prefer to ignore the influence of individual sin while focusing exclusively on the inherent goodness of the human heart. Henri found a way to include both realities in his teaching by grounding them in the Eucharist and giving each its proper place in the human experience. Nouwen argued that, while "brokenness" is a reality of our fallen human nature, the "blessing" of being chosen as God's beloved is the deeper truth God seeks to restore through the sacrifice of his Son, Jesus Christ.

While I often feel like my brokenness proves my unlovability and reinforces my self-rejection, there is a better and truer path to take. Henri suggests that when we listen to the voice calling us "beloved," it becomes possible for us to see our brokenness as an opportunity to grow closer to Christ and to the blessing God has given us. In this way, what once fed our self-rejection has become a pathway to deeper communion. What felt like punishment has been received as careful pruning.

❋ ❋ ❋

The story of Zacchaeus the tax collector in Luke's gospel speaks to us about this deep truth of who we are and how God perceives us even in our brokenness and sin. Luke points out that Zacchaeus was "short in stature" and therefore had to climb a tree in order to see Jesus above the crowd. I wonder if there is a metaphorical correlation between the smallness of Zacchaeus and his life's work as an unjust tax collector who gained wealth by taking from the poor. When our brokenness defines us, we live very small lives. Our worldview and how we relate to neighbors and friends become small and punitive. We see everything around us, including ourselves, through the lens of our brokenness. Zacchaeus may have had a big bank account, but he was "a small man" in many ways, which is why he was desperate to see Jesus. Generally speaking, there were two reasons most people in Jesus' time pursued him: they were either desperate for new life or desperate to find a way to kill him. For Zacchaeus, we can safely assume it was the former.

So when Jesus called Zacchaeus out of the tree and essentially said, *"I want to stay at your house tonight,"* it was Jesus' way of saying, *"Even you, Zacchaeus, are the beloved. You are caught up in a deeply broken system in a deeply broken world, but this is not who you really are."*

I've often wondered how difficult it may have been for Zacchaeus to hear those words of love from Jesus. Even for a person of Henri Nouwen's spiritual stature, it could be hard to hear Jesus' words of love: "My tendencies toward self-rejection and self-deprecation make it hard to hear these words truly and let them descend into the center of my heart. But once I have received these words fully, I am set free from my compulsion to prove myself to the world and can live in it without belonging to it. Once I have accepted the truth that I am God's beloved child, unconditionally loved, I can be sent into the world to speak and to act as Jesus did."[28]

The integration of the brokenness and the blessing of our humanity was woven through much of Henri's writing, though he had different ways of describing it. For example, in his book *Intimacy*, Henri uses the language of "light" and "dark"—frequent in the Gospel of John—to describe these same realities:

> It is very difficult for each of us to believe in Christ's words, "I did not come to call the virtuous, but sinners."...To come to an inner unity, totality and wholeness, every part of our self should be accepted and integrated. Christ represents the light in us. But Christ was crucified between two murderers and we cannot deny them, and certainly not the murderers who live in us.[29]

For me, it is this inner unity that is so hard to allow. Mostly I would prefer to avoid emotional pain by choosing to ignore any memory that might release it. The convenience of avoidance is always alluring, but the long-term consequences prove to be much worse than acceptance. There are moments when I can face a deep pain and allow myself to embrace and feel it. In these moments of acceptance, I can sense that this pain belongs, and I understand that it is not so scary after all. I am sometimes afraid that if I allow a camping space for the pain in my heart, it will take over the entire campground, causing the love to flee. But both pain and love can coexist. I realize that the love still remains. Henri believed it is through the intentional practice of solitude and prayer that we are able to encounter the One who loves and accepts us no matter what. For my own journey, these words of Henri are just what I need to remember:

> Our true challenge is to return to the center, to the heart, and to find there the gentle voice that speaks to us and

affirms us in a way no human voice ever could. The basis of all ministry is the experience of God's unlimited and unlimiting acceptance of us as beloved children, an acceptance so full, so total, and all-embracing, that it sets us free from our compulsion to be seen, praised, and admired and frees us for Christ, who leads on the road of service.

This experience of God's acceptance frees us from our needy self and thus creates new space where we can pay selfless attention to others. This new freedom in Christ allows us to move in the world uninhibited by our compulsions and to act creatively even when we are laughed at and rejected, even when our words and actions lead us to death.[30]

For Retreat and Reflection

QUESTIONS TO JOURNAL WITH *(select those that draw you)*

1. Are you convinced in your mind that God loves you completely without conditions? Why or why not? Does your heart trust your belovedness in God's eyes? What strengthens or undermines your trust?

2. Where is your sense of belonging most rooted? Do those roots grow deep down into the soil of God's love, or are they more attached to various identity groups in the world? What imperatives would you write to yourself to help keep you rooted in God's love?

3. What does it mean to you that the "image of God" is implanted in all human beings, including you? How does it help you to value what God clearly cherishes? If this "truest self" is sheer gift, how does it free you to live in this world?

4. Of the five false narratives presented in this chapter, which do you find most seductive? Why? How can you best counter these false messages about who you are? What practices might help you listen more closely to the "voice from the balcony"?

5. When have you known self-rejection? When have you felt genuine self-acceptance of both your gifts and your weaknesses? What have been the fruits of each path?

SPIRITUAL EXERCISES AND PRAYERFUL ACTIONS:
A SELF-GUIDED MEDITATION ON RECEIVING DIVINE LOVE

- Sit quietly in the presence of Jesus. Hear him speak tenderly to you of his heart—the heart of God's immense and endless love for you.

- Whenever you feel resistance, let yourself speak: "But, Lord, I am...." Tell him your fears; share your shame; confess your guilt.

- Each time you object with "But," hear him respond in words like these: "Yes, I understand. And I love you still. You are made in God's love, for God's love, to respond in love. Do not lose heart. You are a work in progress. I am with you always, drawing you into my own heart."

- Let your dialogue flow in this vein until you feel calm and centered. Give thanks.

- Choose a word or phrase from this meditation and carry it with you into the rest of your day.

AND/OR:

In your journal, write a letter of encouragement to yourself as if from the perspective of a wise friend or experienced spiritual guide. What words can quiet the clamor of "voices from the cellar"? What words would you offer from "the balcony voice" that knows clearly who you are?

Note in your calendar to read this letter in a month's time and record what you notice in yourself.

In the Next Chapter...

We have chosen to begin exploring "the art of living" under the theme of identity. Who are we as human beings? Who am I, individually, among so many people? Our true identity is part of a great mystery—the mystery of life itself—which perhaps is why we seem to be psychologically and spiritually "wired" to seek answers to these questions.

Yet questions about our human identity are invariably linked to questions about divine identity. Countless theologians through the centuries have affirmed that knowledge of self and knowledge of God cannot be separated. Once we get clear that our true identity as human beings is found in acknowledging ourselves as sons and daughters of the living God, we naturally begin to turn our attention more directly to the nature of this God in whose image we are made. What does it mean to be children of such a God?

As important as it is to find clarity on *what we are not* (not defined by what we possess, or what we do, or how others think of us), it is equally crucial to come to clarity on *what God is not*. Our images of God can be just as muddled and damaging as our images of ourselves. Here is where, as Christians, we can look to Jesus as the embodiment of God's life and spirit in our world. Jesus gives us a clear lens through which to see the true character of God, the authentic nature of divine being, a living picture of the One "in whom we live and move and have our being" (Acts 17:8). So, we turn to the theme of chapter 2, "God: Discovering the Divine."

CHAPTER TWO

God

Discovering the Divine

The moment you ask the question "How can I find God?" is the very moment you have been found by God. The problem is that we do not believe it is true, so we go searching, as though God is in hiding somewhere and needs to be found. Finding God is really just about awakening to the truth that God has found you.

Addressing God in a meditation, Henri Nouwen writes, "Your heart is open to receive anyone with total, unrestricted love. For anyone who wants to come to you, there is room."[31] Nouwen wants us to realize that finding God involves keeping ourselves open to the precious divinity revealed to us. We are not to ignore the God who makes himself known to us, Nouwen is saying, but to act when God's precious presence comes into view for us. The Scriptures back him up in this claim.

For instance, there is a parable in Scripture in which Jesus tells about a treasure hidden in a field. A man goes out to plow his field. The passage is very short, just one verse, so it lends itself to richly imaginative reading: "The kingdom of heaven is like treasure hidden in a field. When a man found it, he hid it again, and then in his joy went and sold all he had and bought that field" (Matthew 13:44). I like to picture this story in my mind using imaginative liberty in line with Nouwen's writings. Historians of the ancient Middle East remind us that it wasn't uncommon for people to bury their savings for protection. But sometimes people would be forced to leave their land with their treasure still buried, unknown to the public. It's difficult to verify, but there was apparently a law that if you owned a plot of land and found a treasure buried there, then it was yours to keep. So if you were a sharecropper, it would be wise to keep your eyes open for a buried treasure. I imagine the farmer as a sharecropper plowing in another man's field. *Clink*, his plow hits something. The man stops, begins digging around, and guess what? There's a treasure chest there! He breaks open the latch. Unbelievable! Inside are gold coins, all stacked up.

The man looks around to see if anyone is watching, because he doesn't own the field. Being very shrewd, he covers it back up and reburies it. As the parable goes, "When a man found it, he hid it again." The man decides to sell everything he has in order to buy the field because of the value of the treasure he found. Now he's overjoyed, because the treasure is his.

One way to look at this parable is to say that we're the man. We stumble upon the treasure, which is the love of God in Jesus. We go and we sell everything we have—all our personal wishes and dreams—to follow Jesus. But there is another, deeper way of seeing the parable. What if the man plowing in the field is God? And what if you are the treasure? "Come on!" you say. "That's not the way it is supposed to go." Yet elsewhere in the gospels, Jesus tells another story about a man who went and scattered seed in a field. And the man in the story was God. Another story in Luke tells of a shepherd who left ninety-nine sheep and went to look for the one lost one. Who was that shepherd? It was God in Jesus. Still another story tells of a woman who lost her valuable coin. She swept all over the house and turned everything upside down to find it because it meant so much to her. Who was the woman in the parable? It was God in Jesus.

What if you're the treasure in the field, and God came along to dig you up out of the dirt, buy that field, bring you back home, polish you up, and use you for the purposes for which you were designed? Is it hard to think of yourself as such a treasure? Well, it isn't hard for Jesus to think of you that way.

Nouwen says that God is offering a way to find a home designed specifically for us. This is the path to find God. It is not a path of our searching to find a hidden God. God has already done the search. For us, it is the path of awakening to the presence of the One who gave everything, namely, his Son, to bring us home.

WHAT IS GOD LIKE?

Speaking "heart to heart" to God, Nouwen writes, "You want to draw all people to yourself and offer them a home where every human desire is met, every human longing comes to rest and every human need is satisfied."[32]

I once had a conversation with a friend who suggested that atheists have more in common with Jesus than do many Christians. I asked, "Is this because there are many atheists who are good and kind to others, and many Christians who are cruel and judgmental?"

The problem with this comparison, however, is that Christianity is not a moralistic religion. Some people find the grace of Christ in the midst of moral despair, and it takes a long time for one's character to transform. There may be more in common between Jesus and some atheists with regard to morality but not with regard to worldview and faith. Nouwen would say Christianity is not about morality but about unconditional love. Clearly, I was building my counterargument in my head, until my friend surprised me with his answer to my question. He said, "No. The reason atheists have more in common with Jesus than most Christians is that atheists and Jesus both reject the kind of god that does not exist—an always angry and unloving god." Suddenly, I was compelled. He went on to make the case that many Christians functionally believe (or act as though) God is harsh and judgmental. This explains why they behave in harsh and judgmental ways toward others—because they're projecting their image of God into the world in which they live. And both atheists and Jesus reject such a notion of God. A harsh and judgmental God is not what we are seeking in our quest, Nouwen would say, but a compassionate and caring Friend.

The point is that we must not assume that because we profess our faith in the God of the Bible and Christianity, we are not still influenced by counter images to the One True God we are seeking to know, love, trust, and follow. Therefore, it is wise and helpful to our spiritual lives to take time to consider the character of God—what God is like and what God is *not* like.

Nouwen says, "The truly good news is that God is not a distant God, a God to be feared and avoided, a God of revenge, but a God who is moved by our pains and participates in the fullness of the human struggle....God is a compassionate God. This means, first of all, that he is a God who has chosen to be God-with-us....As soon as we call God, 'God-with-us,' we enter into a new relationship of intimacy with him. By calling him Immanuel, we recognize that he has committed himself to live in solidarity with us, to share our joys and pains, to defend and protect us, and to suffer all of life with us. The God-with-us is a close God, a God whom we call our refuge, our stronghold, our wisdom, and even, more intimately, our helper, our shepherd, our love. We will never really know God as a compassionate God if we do not understand with our heart and mind that 'he lived among us' (John 1:14)."[33]

Henri Nouwen grew up in the Netherlands with two loving and supportive parents and all the freedom to enjoy a happy childhood while developing a large imagination for life and God. Nouwen acknowledged that this upbringing, for which he was grateful, allowed him to more easily imagine God as a kind, loving, and generous God than people who grew up with more challenging families of origin. Nevertheless, Nouwen faced spiritual challenges that affected his image of God, causing him to need to find healing himself. Ultimately, Nouwen came to see in the deepest of ways that Jesus offered us the face of God. Jesus helps us to see what God is truly like, namely, that God is near and that God is love.

First, to say that God is near is a statement of both proximity and empathy. God, in Jesus through the Holy Spirit, has come to be with us. In John 20:21–22, when the risen Christ appeared to the disciples, he said to them, "'Peace be with you. As the Father has sent me, so I send you.' Then he breathed on them and said, 'Receive the Holy Spirit.'"

God is near to us in proximity through the Spirit, and God is near to us in his love. The entire story of the Scriptures is the story of a God who is in constant pursuit of humanity, from the moment when Adam and Eve hid themselves in shame in the Garden to the climax of the narrative when God comes as Immanuel, "God-with-us," in Jesus. Then, in Revelation, John writes, "See, the home of God is among mortals. He will dwell with them as their God; they will be his people, and God himself will be with them" (Revelation 21:3). God is near to us because God loves us.

That is the message that Nouwen came to realize and wished to share with a world that so often considers itself unloved. Even for those of us who believe that God is near, we sometimes experience God as distant and feel God's absence. These are times when it is helpful to remember what we truly believe about God, so we can endure the valleys of our experiences and learn the spiritual lessons that can be learned only in those valleys.

Nouwen acknowledged how hard it can be to remember the deep truth of God's nature: "Knowing God's heart means consistently, radically, and very concretely to announce and reveal that God is love and only love, and that every time fear, isolation, or despair begin to invade the human soul this is not something that comes from God. This sounds very simple and maybe even trite, but very few people know that they are loved without any conditions or limits."[34]

One of the great paintings that helped Henri form his robust image of God was Rembrandt's *The Return of the Prodigal Son*. In his book of the same name, Nouwen drew attention to the distinct characteristics of each of the father's hands. One was feminine, one masculine. This helped Nouwen to see God as both loving Mother and loving Father: "He holds, and she caresses. He confirms, and she consoles. He is, indeed, God, in whom both manhood and womanhood, fatherhood and motherhood, are fully present."[35] This image allowed Nouwen to form a fuller image of God, whereby the strength and compassion of God could be held together in paradox.

Drawing from the Letter of 1 John, Nouwen also talks about the unconditional love of God as "God's first love"—that before we loved, God "first loved us" (1 John 4:19). This is in contrast to all the "second loves"—people who try to love us but fail, leaving us disappointed or sometimes deeply hurt. Nouwen suggests that the second loves—the imperfect love of our parents, teachers, friends, coaches, and neighbors—are only able to be a partial reflection of the "first love," the unconditional love of God that is never fading, shifting, or fleeting. This means that though we need the love of people in our lives, we can accept their limitations, too, for we can find our deepest need for love only in the heart of Jesus.

HOW CAN I HEAL MY IMAGE OF GOD?

Nouwen admits, "Most of us distrust God. Most us think of God as a fearful, punitive authority or as an empty, powerless nothing. Jesus' core message was that God is neither a powerless weakling nor a powerful boss, but a lover, whose only desire is to give us what our hearts most desire."[36]

Perhaps one of the decisions for which Henri Nouwen was most revered was his choice to leave the prestige of two decades of teaching at Harvard and Yale to spend the rest of his life serving as a pastor to a community of adults with physical and intellectual disabilities and their assistants at L'Arche Daybreak in Richmond Hill, Ontario. Nouwen did not make this decision in order to be admired but because he was in need of spiritual healing that could not be found in the libraries or lecture halls of the Ivy League. He writes, "My decision to leave Harvard was a difficult one....Finally, I realized that my increasing inner darkness, my feeling of being rejected by some of my students, colleagues, friends, and even God, my inordinate need for affirmation and affection, and my deep sense of not belonging were clear signs that I was not following the way of God's spirit."[37] It was during his time at L'Arche that Nouwen encountered the God who loves for no other reason than that God is beautiful and creates every human being in love and beauty. This image of God needed to replace a false image of a god who demands achievement, success, and accolades. In the presence of people with intellectual disabilities, the ego formed around academic success suddenly had no relevance.

It was with L'Arche residents like his friend Adam, who could neither speak nor move without assistance, where Nouwen had to address the question, "Would God still love me even if I am not perceived as relevant to a competitive world?" Because if the answer was "no," then how could God love Adam? But Henri knew in his mind and heart that God *did* love Adam, so there must have been something about God that Nouwen was missing at Yale. He knew at an intellectual level that the answer had to be "yes," but he also saw deep down that he did not fully believe it. All his energy was fighting against the idea of God's noncompetitive love. This is where the love of God becomes more terrifying than the wrath of God, because when we recognize it clearly, we also see how much of our lives have been built on something false. So, Adam became Nouwen's teacher and healing companion.

Because our images of God shape our view of God, and our view of God in turn affects how we function in the world, it is important that we consider our images of God. No one has a complete or perfect image of God—as the apostle Paul writes, "We see through a glass dimly" (1 Corinthians 13:12)—but we can move in the direction of wholeness. Sometimes our images of God need correction, such as imagining God to be a harsh judge or a distant relative. Sometimes our images of God are not necessarily false but one-sided, and we would benefit from more dimension.

This is why religious art and iconography have been so helpful for Christians through the centuries. When we ponder the way great artists imagine, express, and portray their images of God, we have an opportunity to see things in a new way and thus for healing to take place.

Several years ago, I visited the Catedral Metropolitana de Barranquilla, in Colombia. In the front of the cathedral, raised high up to the focal point of the sanctuary, was a massive statue of a strong and mighty Jesus ascending in victory, with a cross in hand raised up to the heavens. Shackled prisoners, with hands tied together and arms stretched upward at the feet of Jesus, were set free from their prisons and rising with him in victory. The statue is called *Cristo Libertador* or "Christ the Liberator." The image of this statue was seared into my memory. Every time I think of Colombia, the image comes to mind, and I remember the power of the experience of standing beneath it. Contemplating this statue has brought healing to my image of God in a particular way. It took me a few months of pondering to realize the meaning of the effect this statue had on me.

I had spent much of my life contemplating the images of the crucifix and the empty cross. These are critically important images for me because they remind me of the suffering of God on the cross and the forgiveness and hope I have because of this great work. But the problem was that I carried years of false guilt with these images because they were the only ones I had to rely on, and they were formed in me alongside experiences of childhood trauma. So every time I looked at Jesus hanging on a cross, I did not sense the love of God but felt that it was my fault my Lord had to die. I felt only the guilt of my own bad decisions. Then I looked at the empty cross and the promise of eternal life, and my false guilt was driven deeper. Not only did I cause my Lord to die, but now he is giving me an eternal reward. How can I accept that in good conscience? My experiences caused me to feel guilty about nearly everything. Even though I knew God's love and forgiveness for me in Jesus Christ, I still could not forgive myself and accept God's love.

Although this continues to be a lifelong journey for me, the statue of *Cristo Libertador* brought a measure of healing. It showed me that God not only forgives me of my misdeeds but also sets me free from everything that caused me to do those misdeeds, including my fears, my selfishness, my wounds, and even my own guilt. I look back on my life and see a multitude of threats and circumstances from which I believe God delivered me. Then I am reminded that God not only forgives me in the end so I can enjoy eternal life but that God is alive and bringing me salvation every single day. There is nothing for me to fear, because I am being set free by the One who rules in love over all creation. In Jesus, God's love is mighty and powerful, and all are blessed to live in the freedom Christ provides.

As I mentioned before, one of the most powerful healing images for Nouwen was Rembrandt's *The Return of the Prodigal Son*. On a trip to France, Henri visited Trosly, where he stumbled upon a reproduction of this painting, which inspired him to see the original in St. Petersburg. The image was so powerful for him that he wrote a masterful interpretation of the parable and the painting inspired by it. The painting guides Nouwen's reflection and represents the heart of his book *The Return of the Prodigal Son*. Nouwen writes, "The true center of Rembrandt's painting is the hands of the father. On them all the light is concentrated; on them the eyes of the bystanders are focused; in them mercy becomes flesh; upon them forgiveness, reconciliation, and healing come together, and, through them, not only the tired son, but also the worn-out father find their rest."[38]

Nouwen unlocks the meaning of the parable and unleashes the

power of the painting by relating the dynamics of both painting and parable to his own life of desolation, resentment, reconciliation, and renewal. Henri needed to see, through the hands of the father, that God's strength does not minimize God's tenderness, nor does God's tenderness discount God's strength. In fact, the compassion of God holds the strength and tenderness together. This recovery of a fuller image of God offered Henri the imagination to seek to live his own life in the same way. He writes:

> Perhaps the most radical statement Jesus ever made is: "Be compassionate as your Father is compassionate." God's compassion is described by Jesus not simply to show me how willing God is to feel for me, or to forgive my sins and offer me new life and happiness, but to invite me to become like God and to show the same compassion to others as he is showing to me....
>
> What I am called to make true is that whether I am the younger or the elder son, I am the son of my compassionate Father. I am an heir. No one says it more clearly than Paul when he writes: "The Spirit himself joins with our spirit to bear witness that we are children of God. And if we are children, then we are heirs, heirs of God and joint heirs with Christ, provided that we share his sufferings, so as to share his glory." Indeed, as son and heir I am to become successor. I am destined to step into my Father's place and offer to others the same compassion that he has offered me. The return to the Father is ultimately the challenge to become the Father.[39]

When we take time to reflect on our images of God with the intention of seeking healing and growth, we find that God seems to become bigger than we first imagined, and we can let go of small images of God that no longer serve us. In doing so, we become more like the God we are seeking to imagine.

WHAT DOES GOD WANT FROM ME?

Nouwen writes:

> I am growing in the awareness that God wants my whole life, not just part of it. It is not enough to give just so much time and attention to God and keep the rest for myself. It is not enough to pray often and deeply and then move from there to my own projects....
>
> To return to God means to return to God with all that I am and all that I have. I cannot return to God with just half of my being. As I reflected this morning again on the story of the prodigal son and tried to experience myself in the embrace of the father, I suddenly felt a certain resistance to being embraced so fully and totally. I experienced not only a desire to be embraced, but also a fear of losing my independence. I realized that God's love is a jealous love. God wants not just a part of me, but all of me. Only when I surrender myself completely to God's parental love can I expect to be free from endless distractions, ready to hear the voice of love, and able to recognize my own unique call.[40]

I'll never forget one February night, at the age of sixteen, when the trajectory of my life took a 180-degree turn for the better. I was at the bottom of the darkest season of my life to this day. Struggling with suicidal thoughts, running with a gang that was centered on violence and drug abuse, my life was unraveling at a terrifying pace. On this night I sat on my windowsill and cried out in pain and fury to the God I thought I knew as a child. I held nothing back, even questioning the existence of God. By the time morning came, a sense of peace and love came over me that I had never known until that night. I knew that everything was going to be all right, and that somehow God was present and had something to do with this nearly miraculous change of heart.

The only thing I knew to do was to call my friend Eric, whose life clearly had become centered around Jesus. Eric was a young and vibrant believer who led teenage Bible studies on Saturday nights, went on mission trips with his church youth group, and sought to live his life intentionally with the love of Jesus at the center. Eric quickly came over to my house, gave me a big hug, and handed me a booklet called *My Heart, Christ's Home*. I asked him what had happened the previous night, and Eric said, "You became a Christian last night." I was confused. I responded, "But I've been a Catholic my whole life. What do you mean I became a Christian?" He said, "Well, now it's real. You accepted Christ into the center of your life and decided to follow Jesus." "I did?" "Yes." "What does that mean?" And Eric said, "Come to our youth fellowship gathering at my church and you'll see." So, I did, and from that moment on I have been intentionally following Jesus.

On that particular night, the transcendent God I knew as a child became immanent for me. That is, the God who created the entire cosmos became the God who also wanted to be my friend. It wasn't that I became a Christian that night but that I simply awakened to the availability of an intimate God of love in all times and places. No longer was God confined to worship or the parish building, but God could be accessed in my bedroom at night, in the ocean or mountains, in conversations with friends, on the soccer field, and even at school.

That night was a homecoming for me. But over time I've come to see that all of life is a homecoming journey that never fully reaches its destination in this life. We are always on our way home back to God, which is what God ultimately wants most from us: to come home.

Rembrandt's image of *The Return of the Prodigal Son* was deeply important to Nouwen because in the image of the father he could see the essence of the gospel and the meaning of his own life. Nouwen writes:

> For most of my life I have struggled to find God, to know God, to love God. I have tried hard to follow the guidelines of the spiritual life—pray always, work for others, read the Scriptures—and to avoid the many temptations to dissipate myself. I have failed many times but always tried again, even when I was close to despair.
>
> Now I wonder whether I have sufficiently realized that during all this time God has been trying to find me, to know me, and to love me. The question is not "How am I to find God?" but "How am I to let myself be found by him?" The question is not "How am I to know God?" but "How am I to let myself be known by God?" And, finally, the question is not "How am I to love God?" but "How am I to let myself be loved by God?" God is look-

ing into the distance for me, trying to find me, and longing to bring me home.[41]

As the story is recorded in Luke's gospel, the younger of the two sons takes his share of their benevolent and wealthy father's inheritance and runs off to squander the money in reckless and pleasure-seeking activities, only to find himself at rock bottom in a pigsty. When he "came to himself" (Luke 15:17), he prepares his apology and plans to work off the debt. So he stumbles his way back to the father's home. When the father sees his son off in the distance, he does what no wealthy father would have done in those days: he picks up his cloak, baring his legs, and runs to greet his lost son. When the father finally embraces him, he wants none of the son's repayment options. He only wants to celebrate his son's return.

No matter what our experience has been, no matter where we've wandered off, whether by our choices or the choices of others or some combination of both, the God who made us and sustains our lives simply wants us home in his presence. This is where we belong. Such homecoming is not simply an improved moral performance. After all, there are two sons in the story. The elder cannot be morally outper-formed, but he is as distant from the father's heart as was the younger son. Again, the point is not performance but a relationship of love and intimacy.

Henri Nouwen wrote repeatedly about this concept of homecom-ing in the spiritual life. In his book *Lifesigns: Intimacy, Fecundity, and Ecstasy in Christian Perspective*, Nouwen writes about how God wants, first of all, for us to be in communion with God and others—the invitation to "intimacy." Second, God wants us to be open to change in order that we may live fruitful lives—the call to "fecundity."

Third, God wants us to receive his promise of joy—the gift of "ecstasy."

Nouwen suggests that the invitation to communion with God and others requires that we move from the "house of fear" to the "house of love." Both fear and love are less like simple emotions and more like places in which we choose to take up residence. It's not that we are simply afraid of one thing and not another, but as Henri's observes, fear "has become an obvious dwelling place, an acceptable basis on which to make our decisions and plan our lives."[42] Henri goes on to flesh out the many ways in which fear can (sometimes subtly) dominate our general posture in the world, because fear begets fear. Therefore, we cannot reason our way out of fear. The only way out of fear is through love. As we are reminded in 1 John 4:18, "There is no fear in love, but perfect love casts out fear."

Henri suggests that a key spiritual movement is the "movement out of the house of fear into the house of love."[43] He writes: "Why is there no reason to fear any longer? Jesus himself answers this question succinctly when he approaches his frightened disciples walking on the lake: 'It is I. Do not be afraid' (John 6:20). The house of love is the house of Christ, the place where we can think, speak, and act in the way of God—not in the way of a fear-filled world. From this house the voice of love keeps calling out: 'Do not be afraid...come and follow me...see where I live....take for your heritage the Kingdom prepared for you since the foundation of the world.'"[44]

God wants us to not be afraid. What does that mean for us? It means we don't give in to our fears but instead turn away from them. When fears come our way, they can be overcome with the love of Christ residing within us. There is no fear that is stronger than God, and there is no love that is greater than the Lord's. The goal throughout our lives should be to lean into God's love and never be pulled away from it.

HOW AM I FOUND BY GOD?

Nouwen writes: "It is very difficult for each of us to believe in Christ's words, 'I did not come to call the virtuous, but sinners....' Perhaps no psychologist has stressed the need of self-acceptance as the way to self-realization so much as Carl Jung. For Jung, self-realization meant the integration of the shadow. It is the growing ability to allow the dark side of our personality to enter into our awareness and thus prevent a one-sided life in which only that which is presentable to the outside world is considered as a real part of ourselves. To come to an inner unity, totality and wholeness, every part of our self should be accepted and integrated. Christ represents the light in us. But Christ was crucified between two murderers and we cannot deny them, and certainly not the murderers who live in us."[45]

A few years ago, I was in Hong Kong on a study trip with some colleagues. Three of us were having dinner, and one minister in the group was telling a story about a church member she was trying to help through some relational problems. The church member, a young woman, kept bouncing around from one relationship to another. She was hoping to marry her most recent beau right away and wanted her minister to perform the ceremony. But our friend wasn't feeling good about performing the wedding without more time for the couple to work on what seemed already to be a disastrous relationship. The young woman admitted, "I'm just really afraid of being lonely." In her wisdom, our minister friend, who was not afraid to tell people what she thought, said in response, "Unless you become okay with being alone, no number of relationships, no kind of relationship, no other human being will be able to fill that void." She continued, "You have to become okay with being alone first before you can really enter into a serious and mature relationship."

I thought her very wise. Like the young woman she spoke truth to, many of us are so afraid of being lonely that we can't rest with ourselves alone. Yet until we "become okay with being alone," we can't learn more fully who we are. Nouwen refers to the wisdom of Carl Jung in accepting and integrating the whole of our life, shadow and light. Fear of being in solitude prevents us from seeing the wounds and shadows we could bring to God's light for healing. These unconscious wounds interfere with healthy relationships. We want to have vibrant relationships that are life-giving and fulfilling. But as long as we flee our shadow side, we remain lonely in our relationships with others and homesick for God.

There are two primary theological reasons why we find ourselves homesick for God. The first is that we're made in the divine image. God is reason, will, intelligence—and we share in those qualities as a result. God is also Trinity, existing as communion in constant self-giving love among Father, Son, and Holy Spirit. It's not that God is a separate individual who may or may not be interested in relationship. No! God *is* relationship. The apostle John says that God is love (1 John 4:8), and love cannot exist apart from relationship. Love exists only between persons, in relationship. Since we are made in the image of God, we are designed for communion. We are made to be in harmony with God and all creation. That is what *shalom* is—the harmony of all things.

The second truth is related to the first. We're made in God's image but born into a broken world. And in this broken world we don't know how to give love. We don't even know how to receive love. When we are wounded, our love gets distorted and our pain gets transmitted rather than transformed. So we walk through this broken world, made for harmonious, loving, and life-giving relationships, but broken nonetheless. Not being loved well or loving well is a root cause of loneliness. Some of us know loneliness more deeply than others.

What do we do with our homesickness and loneliness? Often, sadly, what we do is try to fill the emptiness with other things. When I experience loneliness, I distract myself. I feel a sharp pain, the stab of loneliness; rather than entering into it and letting it teach me about myself, or letting the pain of my loneliness move me out of myself to give love to someone else, I evade my feelings and distract myself. I get on Facebook or Instagram or watch a Netflix show. Some people turn to alcohol, to gossip, or to overworking. Others go shopping to comfort themselves with "retail therapy."

Henri Nouwen reminds us that God is not simply an additional source of stimuli that we add to our quiver of distractions. One of his prayers speaks to this truth:

> Dear God,
> I am so afraid to open my clenched fists!
> Who will I be when I have nothing left to hold on to?
> Who will I be when I stand before you with empty hands?
> Please help me to gradually open my hands and to discover that I am not what I own, but what you want to give me.[46]

Blaise Pascal once said, "All of humanity's problems stem from one source: our inability to sit quietly in our own room for an hour."[47] Think about that. If you turned off all sources of stimulation, all sources of distraction, could you just sit in your room, by yourself, doing nothing, for one hour, and be content?

If you can't, it doesn't mean you're bad or there's something wrong with you any more than with anyone else. It means that you've got a loneliness problem. You keep trying to find solace in your pain through some kind of distraction.

Henri Nouwen said it like this:

> To live a spiritual life we must first find the courage to enter into the desert of our loneliness and to change it by gentle and persistent efforts into a garden of solitude. This requires not only courage but also a strong faith. As hard as it is to believe that the dry desolate desert can yield endless varieties of flowers, it is equally hard to imagine that our loneliness is hiding unknown beauty. The movement from loneliness to solitude, however, is the beginning of any spiritual life because it is a movement from the restless senses to the restful spirit, from the outward-reaching cravings to the inward-reaching search, from the fearful clinging to the fearless play.[48]

Our faith invites us to search inwardly, to go on the inward journey in order to get to know ourselves in the deep, protected corners of our hearts. What we find is that when we go inward with sincere faith, the journey will then lead us upward. This is because the One who brought your loneliness to the cross is the same One who promises to meet you there in that same place of pain. This is why Jesus says, "Abide in me as I abide in you" (John 15:4). There's a big difference between believing in Christ and abiding in Christ. We are not called merely to cognitive belief in him. We are called to be immersed in his life. God is an ocean, and we're a thimble. You can't put the ocean into a thimble, but you can put the thimble into the ocean. Solitude is our practice of being with God alone. When we practice solitude, we quickly discover how dependent we are on external stimuli. Without the many distractions of our daily lives, we sometimes feel anxious and tense. When nobody speaks to us, calls on us, or needs our help, we may begin to feel insignificant. Then we wonder whether we are useful, valuable, and relevant. Our temptation is to leave this fearful solitude quickly and get busy again to reassure ourselves that we are valuable. But that is a temptation, because what makes us valuable is not another's response to us but God's everlasting love for us.

Abba Moses, one of the ancient Desert Fathers, said this to a monk: "Go, sit in your cell and your cell will teach you everything."[49] Most of us do not live like monks in "cells" or solitary rooms. But we can learn from their way of life and incorporate their practices in some ways into our modern experience. Spiritual teachers have long known that coming face to face with yourself is one of the greatest learning opportunities we can have. Spiritual teacher Jim Finley talks about having a "daily rendezvous with God," where you take a moment out of each day to enter solitude and deep listening.

Nouwen writes:

> When God has become our shepherd, our refuge, our fortress, then we can reach out to him in the midst of a broken world and feel at home while still on the way. When God dwells in us, we can enter in a wordless dialogue with him while still waiting on the day that he will lead us into the house where he has prepared a place for

us (John 14:2). Then we can wait while we have already arrived and ask while we have already received. Then, indeed, we can comfort each other with the words of Paul.

"There is no need to worry; but if there is anything you need, pray for it, asking God for it with prayer and thanksgiving, and that peace of God, which is so much greater than we can understand, will guard your hearts and your thoughts, in Christ Jesus." (Philippians 4:6–7)[50]

HOW DO I MOVE FROM FEAR TO FAITH?

Nouwen writes: "'Do not be afraid, have no fear,' is the voice we most need to hear. This voice was heard by Zechariah when Gabriel, the angel of the Lord, appeared to him in the temple and told him that his wife Elizabeth would bear a son; this voice was heard by Mary when the same angel entered her house in Nazareth and announced that she would conceive, bear a child, and name him Jesus; this voice was also heard by the women who came to the tomb and saw that the stone was rolled away. 'Do not be afraid, do not be afraid, do not be afraid.' The voice uttering these words sounds all through history as the voice of God's messengers, be they angels or saints. It is the voice that announces a whole new way of being, a being in the house of love, the house of the Lord....

The house of love is not simply a place in the afterlife, a place in heaven beyond this world. Jesus offers us this house right in the midst of our anxious world."[51]

The story of Jesus calming the storm is among the most well-known gospel passages dealing with fear. According to St. Mark, it has been another long and exhausting day of ministry for Jesus. So he and his disciples set out on the Sea of Galilee to get away from the crowds and find some rest. Jesus was so tired that he fell asleep in the stern before a terrible storm arose. The sky grew dark, the winds began to howl, and the waves crashed against and into the boat. The disciples, experienced fishermen on the Sea of Galilee, were struck by fear and terror for their lives. You may have had an experience of naked fear in your own life. Dietrich Bonhoeffer once described the experience of naked fear as the closest thing to the manifestation of evil in this life. It must have been a terrible storm!

We might imagine Jesus cuddled up against a cushion in the back of the boat, dreaming about the next table he wants to build. His panicked disciples rouse him and cry out, "Teacher, don't you care that we are perishing?" (Mark 4:38). This is the first of three important questions in the story.

Henri Nouwen suggests that we are so gripped by fear that it pervades everything. He writes, "We are fearful people. The more people I come to know and the more I come to know people, the more I am overwhelmed by the negative power of fear. It often seems that fear has invaded every part of our being to such a degree that we no longer know what a life without fear would feel like. There always seems to be something to fear: something within us or around us, something close or far away, something visible or invisible, something in ourselves, in others, or in God."[52]

If you are a person who prays, it's then that you look to Jesus your captain and say, "Teacher, don't you care that we are perishing?" Notice the disciples' question is not, "Jesus, can you do something about this?" They know what Jesus can do.

Jesus gets up in response to this prayer. He awakens in the midst of the storm. This is really important. Jesus does not prevent the storm. He awakens in the midst of the storm; we prefer if Jesus kept us from storms, but his purpose is to be present through the storms. Henri Nouwen writes, "As we keep our eyes directed at the One who says, 'Do not be afraid,' we may slowly let go of our fear. We will learn to live in a world without zealously defended borders. We will be free to see the suffering of other people, free to respond not with defensiveness, but with compassion, with peace, with ourselves."[53]

At this point in the story, Jesus looks at the disciples and asks a second question in the text: "Why are you afraid? Have you no faith?" Again, faith does not prevent storms. Faith allows us to face our fears in the midst of the storms. Faith frees us from the tyranny of our fears. The kind of faith Jesus is talking about here is not a body of theological doctrine. It is not even faith in whether this story actually happened as the text recorded it. Personally, I do believe that it happened, but for me it is easy to believe. If God can create the universe and Jesus can rise from the dead, calming a sea is not so difficult to believe. What is hard to believe is that it *still* happens—that it can happen now when our lives are caught in the storm.

This is why we need faith. Faith is a way of seeing that the incarnation of the Creator of heaven and earth, the One who rules the seas, is in our boat. Do you see the joy of this image? You are not lost at sea alone. The Savior is in your boat, and he is there because he loves you. Here once again we discover the grace of Jesus. You are invited to come back home to a God who is overjoyed because in Christ Jesus he has found you and brought you home, and he is not going to let you go. It doesn't matter where your boat heads. He will go with you. The Savior is with you because he delights in you. As you see this, you can become unafraid when the storm comes.

I have never succeeded in talking someone out of being afraid. I cannot even talk myself out of being afraid. According to 1 John, only "perfect love casts out fear." Henri Nouwen knew this deeply. He wrote: "The greatest block in the spiritual life is fear. Prayer, meditation, and education cannot come forth out of fear. God is perfect love, and as John the Evangelist writes, 'Perfect love drives out fear' (1 John 4:18). Jesus' central message is that God loves us with an unconditional love and desires our love, free from all fear, in return."[54]

Anyone who's been a parent knows how this works. You hold the child until she is no longer thinking about monsters but about being held by the loving care of Mom or Dad. Perfect love casts out fear. This is why we turn to God in solitude. Solitude is like running into the Father's bedroom in the middle of the night to receive his warm embrace. Nouwen constantly encouraged his readers to spend time in solitude for this reason. He writes: "Solitude is the place where we can reach the profound bond that is deeper than the emergency bonds of fear and anger. Although fear and anger can indeed drive us together, they cannot give rise to a common witness. In solitude we can come to the realization that we are not driven together but brought together. In solitude we come to know our fellow human beings not as partners who can satisfy our deepest needs, but as brothers and sisters with whom we are called to give visibility to God's all-embracing love."[55]

After Jesus has calmed the storm, we get the third question: the disciples look at each other and say, "Who is this that even the wind and sea obey him?" No matter how long you have known Jesus, there is more to him than you know.

At this point, the disciples' fear over the storm has been transformed into awe at being in the presence of the Savior. "Awe" is also a fear of God. It is the only fear the Bible allows us to have. If we truly recognize the awesomeness of God all around us, then we are not going to fear anything else. As theologians have noted, if you do not fear the God above you, you will fear everything around you.

To be clear, we do not fear God for his judgment. That has all been resolved on the cross. We fear God for his love, because God's love will change our life. God's kindness leads us to repentance. God's love will cause us to let go of personal attachments and our own dreams, out of love for others. The foot of the cross is where all that separates us from God is removed and we become one with God through Jesus. The cross is where we find God in his truest form and where our faith in him is made most real.

For Retreat and Reflection

QUESTIONS TO JOURNAL WITH *(select those that draw you)*

1. If someone asked you what God is like, how would you answer? How have your ways of thinking about God changed over the course of your life? Who or what has most influenced these changes?

2. Name a few false or inadequate images of God you have struggled with in your life. How comfortable are you balancing masculine and feminine characteristics in the divine nature? Is there a work of art, a poem, or a song that has helped you expand your image of God? If so, how?

3. With which character do you most easily identify in the parable of the prodigal son, and why? Who is most difficult to identify

with, and why? What do your responses tell you about your relationship to "spiritual homecoming"?

4. In what ways have you experienced solitude as an opportunity to deepen both your self-understanding and your relationship with God? What fears prevent you from putting your "thimble" into God's "ocean"?

5. What experience do you have of moving from "the house of fear" to "the house of love"? What helps your heart to open to that perfect love that casts out fear?

SPIRITUAL EXERCISES AND PRAYERFUL ACTIONS

- Over the coming days, pay attention to messages about God that you see or hear from media, entertainment, churches, or other aspects of culture. Name the unhelpful images of God you have absorbed, even subtly. In your journal, write some ways in which the character of Jesus challenges and corrects such images.

AND/OR:

The great Quaker John Woolman once had a vision in which he saw an enormous dark sea comprised of the whole of human sin and suffering. Upon crying out to God in anguish, the Spirit showed him an ocean far more vast—an unending ocean of Light—covering the sea of darkness entirely. Imagine this vision. Let your own wounds and fears enter the dark sea. Watch the ocean of Light come over you, and feel its love washing your fears away. Give thanks, and trust the spiritual reality of this vision.

In the Next Chapter...

We have spent some time exploring our understandings and images of God. Of course, we can never arrive at a perfectly clear and comprehensive image of the immense Divine Mystery. Much trouble and conflict arise in human life when people become convinced that they have a lock on truth along with the authority to compel others to believe as they do. Yet while we can never claim to know God fully, some images of divine being are far more adequate and life-giving than others. As Christians, we look to Jesus to provide an authentic picture of God's nature and character.

When we see God through the lens of Jesus' life and teaching, we can scarcely fail to recognize that love lies at the heart of divinity. While some theologians identify unlimited power or knowledge as the pinnacle of Deity (omnipotence or omniscience), many others have seen love as the reigning attribute of God. Among these are some of the church's earliest theologians, who taught that while God's essence cannot be known, God's love energies are everywhere present through the whole of creation. "No one has ever seen the essence of God, but we believe in the essence because we experience the energy," writes St. Basil (fourth century CE). Following in this tradition ten centuries later, one Greek theologian assures us: "The most important thing that happens between God and the human soul is to love and to be loved."[56]

It is the nature of Love to go out of itself—to be fulfilled in the enjoyment of communion with the Beloved. And just as God shares love with all creation, most especially with those created in the *imago Dei*, so God enjoins us to share the same love with each other. We are made by love, for love. "Beloved, let us love one another, because love is from God" (1 John 4:7). Exploring the theme of love—God's love for us, and ours for God and others—is the subject of our next chapter. Fittingly, this chapter lies at the center of our book.

CHAPTER THREE

Love

Experiencing Deep Connection

"Love" is one of the most complicated words in the English language. As the first choice for a hyperbolic positive sentiment about anything, it is grossly overused and confusing: "I love pizza" or "I love going to the movies." How can this be the same word to describe how I feel about my children? To be sure, our experiences with love are immensely varied. Part of what makes the notion of "love" so complex is the way we use it to describe both feelings and behaviors.

At our core, we want to love and be loved because love is the essence of our being. The reason we are drawn to anything that offers us the promise of love is that love is the primary reason this world was formed. The Garden of Eden is an image of the perfect expression of God's love at the dawn of creation.

Henri Nouwen wrote extensively about the subject of love as he wrestled deeply and personally with the love of God, self, and others. For Henri, love is the essence of God himself, such that whenever love is shared, God is present. Henri also knew that pain is not the opposite of love. Fear is the converse of love. But pain or even anger can be the expression of love gone awry. When we experience pain and anger, love is very near.

TO LOVE AND BE LOVED

Those you have deeply loved become part of you. The longer you live, there will always be more people to be loved by you and to become part of your inner community. The wider your inner community becomes, the more easily you will recognize your own brothers and sisters in the strangers around you. Those who are alive within you will recognize those who are alive around you. The wider the community of your heart, the wider the community around you. Thus the pain of rejection, absence, and death can become fruitful. Yes, as you love deeply the ground of your heart will be broken more and more, but you will rejoice in the abundance of the fruit it will bear.[57]

When I was twenty-four years old, a significant and unexpected journey was about to begin for me that would shape my view of God, the world, and myself for the rest of my life. In this year, I got the news that I had contracted stage III testicular cancer. My wife, Devon, and I had been married for a year, I was a student at Fuller Seminary, and I was applying for a youth minister position at my local Presbyterian church. Serving on a volunteer basis at the church already, I had a desk in the church office. I left my desk one day to visit the doctor about a rash on my back. When I admitted that it had been over five years since I'd had a physical, the doctor examined me and discovered a tumor on my left testicle. After leaving the doctor, I called my wife to share the difficult news. The next day I went into surgery to have the tumor removed and analyzed. Two days later I went in for

CT scans of my entire body. The day after that, I received the results that my tumor was a seminoma (the kind that spreads), and the scans lit up throughout my body. The cancer had metastasized in multiple places below my neck. Devon and I met with the local oncologist who recommended an intense chemotherapy treatment at City of Hope Cancer Treatment Center in Duarte, California.

I was scared but hopeful. Mostly I felt frustrated, assuming that I couldn't serve as a Christian ministry leader in such a condition. I was afraid I had lost my opportunity to respond to what I believed was God's call in my life. Even though I still had confidence that God was right by my side, I felt confused.

The day after receiving this burdensome news, I went back to visit the senior pastor at the church to request removal from their hiring process, due to the likelihood that I would not be as available as I had intended when applying for the position. I was devastated and shaken because I really wanted to be their youth minister. As I walked down the church hallway toward the pastor's study, the pastor was on his way to my desk to offer me the position for which I had applied, and our paths crossed. I said, "Pastor Jack, I got some bad news the other day that I need to share with you because I think it disqualifies me from the position." "What happened?" Jack asked. I explained that I had stage III testicular cancer and that I would have to get intensive chemotherapy at City of Hope. There I would reside for a week at a time, receiving a cocktail of three chemotherapy medications, morning and evening, and then return home to recover for two weeks before the next round, probably needing four rounds. This being the case, I felt I should remove myself from the church's hiring process.

Pastor Jack had a look of confusion on his face, as if he wasn't making the connection between this news and the job opportunity.

He expressed great concern for my health at such a young age. He expressed concern about my survival and our future family plans. But he did not express concern about the job. In fact, he said, "Your call to ministry is not predicated on your physical health." I was dumbfounded by his love and acceptance.

In the months that followed, I learned much about the mutuality of love. When I first accepted God's call to ministry, I expected to be the one who would give out love to the congregation I served; I did not expect to learn the importance and challenge of receiving love. As I began my new job of ministering to youth, I would spend a week at City of Hope Cancer Treatment Center, two hours from home, followed by two weeks of recovery at home. When I was home, I would lead the youth group, teach about faith in Jesus Christ, and mentor teenagers in the faith. When I was at City of Hope, teenagers and their parents would come to visit, decorate the off-campus hospital apartment with bright colors, and bring food for my wife and me. I would wheel my hydration bag over to the hospital in the morning and evening to receive my infusion treatments. When my hair fell out, the boys in the youth group shaved their heads to show solidarity. This would become the essence of ministry for me, and still is—seventeen years later—giving and receiving the love of Christ within a worshipping community of faith.

It was a gift of grace for me to discover this mutuality, because it caused me to be dependent on the community I was serving for my own support. I needed them as much as they needed me. I had to deal with my own aversion to being someone in need. At first, I just wanted to give love and not "use" the church to meet my needs. After all, I was called to serve them, not to be served by them. But I learned, paradoxically, that receiving love is actually just another way of giving love. In receiving the care of the community, it was as if they could hear me say: "You have something precious to offer. You have the love of God within you to share, even with me. I realize this enough to make myself vulnerable to your care and love." They recognized that I was loving them by receiving their loving care for me. This led to a beautiful season of ministry as mutual love. Had I not loved them in return through my formation and teaching ministry, their loving care for me would have grown weary. Had I not received their love for me, they would have been kept at a "safe distance," and my teaching would not have reached the same depth of their hearts.

Love is by nature mutual. If we want to give it, we must be willing to receive it. If we want to receive it, we must be willing to give it as well. Our knowledge of such mutuality is limited but real. We can perhaps name family and friends whom we love so much that we want to give all we have to them and they want to give all they have to us. Such experiences are reflections of a much greater divine love. Theologically, the reason love is mutual is because it is wrapped up in the personhood of God as Trinity. "God is love," 1 John tells us. Is not the reverse also true, that "love is God"? God as Trinity exists in a perfectly mutual relationship of giving and receiving love among the three persons of the Godhead. St. Paul's classic benediction expresses this dynamic flow: "The grace of the Lord Jesus Christ and the love of God and the fellowship of the Holy Spirit be with you all" (2 Corinthians 13:14). When we give love and receive love, we are caught up in the essential life of God in all its fullness, fellowship, and grace.

During my season of cancer, seminary studies included Henri Nouwen as core curriculum for several of my courses. Henri helped me understand the inseparable connection between giving and receiving love. His words resonated with my experience: "The more you have loved and have allowed yourself to suffer because of your love, the more you will be able to let your heart grow wider and deeper. When your love is truly giving and receiving, those whom you love will not leave your heart even when they depart from you."[58]

In these words Henri recognized not only the mutuality of love but the integral connection between love and suffering. Henri could sound fierce when it came to love:

> It is like a plow that breaks the ground to allow the seed to take root and grow into a strong plant. Every time you experience the pain of rejection, absence, or death, you are faced with a choice. You can become bitter and decide not to love again, or you can stand straight in your pain and let the soil on which you stand become richer and more able to give life to new seeds.[59]

LOOKING FOR LOVE IN ALL THE WRONG PLACES

Henri Nouwen lived his final years serving adults with physical and intellectual disabilities in Ontario. Many of Nouwen's earlier writings depicted a relentless searching. It was a search he tried to satisfy by becoming ordained in the Catholic church as a priest, by getting a PhD, by serving as a seminary professor at Yale and later at Harvard, by leaving seminary and becoming a temporary monk at a monastery in Genesee, and by serving as a missionary in South America. Through these many experiences, he wrote profound books describing what he was learning about the spiritual life. But if he found what he was looking for, it came to him through the little fellowship at L'Arche Daybreak in Richmond Hill, Ontario.

During his first year there, Nouwen spent the first two hours of every day caring for a man named Adam, who had severe disabilities and could not speak. Henri would wake Adam, get him washed and dressed, take him to breakfast and eat beside him. Then he would bring Adam to the place where he spent the day. At first Nouwen was afraid of this assignment, thinking it would be overwhelming. But before long he began to look forward to it, as he always received a glimpse of the love of Jesus in the eyes of Adam.

People asked Henri if this was the best way for him to make an impact, given his academic training and the fact that his writings were read by hundreds of thousands. Daybreak was so small, and his relationship with Adam such a tiny circle—just a searching scholar and a disabled man who could not speak. But Nouwen explained that he didn't spend time with Adam to make a big splash. He did it because Jesus led him there. He did it because it was freeing to be in a place where people's handicaps were obvious, and he could deal with his own hidden handicaps. He did it for the compassion he received as much as for the compassion he gave. And he did it because after all his searching, it was where he had finally found joy. In Nouwen's own words, "Joy is the secret gift of compassion. We keep forgetting it and thoughtlessly look elsewhere. But each time we return to where there is pain, we get a new glimpse of the joy that is not of this world."[60]

Looking for joy apart from pain is like searching for pain-free love. To love at all is to know the suffering of love lost, wounded, or withdrawn. Yet we resist the pain, often seeking "love" that merely soothes our feelings of emptiness or insecurity. And we tend to look for this love in places or relationships that cannot possibly fulfill our longing—"in all the wrong places."

Where do we imagine we will find acceptance and love? In knowledge, competence, notoriety, success, sensations, pleasure, dreams, or artificially induced states of consciousness? Some seek love in uncommitted sexual relationships. Others look for a sense of belonging and significance in "tribal" groups of racial, ethnic, religious, or ideological purity. Some take social media "likes" or "tweets" for love. These are all superficial, temporary sources of affirmation and security.

A Scripture story comes to mind that speaks to our condition. Early in John's gospel, we find John the Baptist pointing his followers to "one who is coming after me" yet "ranks ahead of me because he was before me" (see John 1:27–30). The Baptist points to Jesus and names him "the lamb of God who takes away the sin of the world." At this point, Peter's brother Andrew and an unnamed friend turn from following John the Baptist to following Jesus. When Jesus realizes he is being followed, he turns, looks at them, and utters his first words recorded in John's gospel: "What are you looking for?" Truly, a question for the ages!

As readers, we are meant to hear this question echoing down the centuries for ourselves. What are we looking for in life? Safety? Prosperity? Recognition? Freedom from guilt? A chance to use our gifts? What deeper desires are motivating this quest called life? Through his question to these two disciples, Jesus is asking us, two millennia later: "What are you really looking for? What is your soul searching to find, such that you would be following after me?" I find it a bit troubling that the one who is supposed to have the answers is the one asking the question. It is an invitation to self-examination. What is our heart truly longing for, in comparison to what we *think* we want in life?

Until we can identify the "what" of our seeking, we cannot really discern the "where" of finding it. I would like to suggest, as Henri did, that what we are looking for is infinite love. But we often don't recognize this as our heart's deepest desire. For example, we might think we are looking for prosperity. We imagine that more material comfort and enjoyment will help us feel successful, accomplished, and proud of ourselves. Wealth and status go hand in hand in our culture. A big fortune makes us feel important. But will this make us feel loved by an infinite love? Of course not! Why is it that some wealthy people seem content, generous, and happy, while others seem so pinched and frustrated with life? It is because wealth has nothing to say to us about feeling infinitely loved. At best, it can give superficial comfort and perhaps prolong our days on earth, but it cannot cause us to feel infinitely loved.

Or we might think we are looking for popularity. We want lots of friends and people who like us, maybe even look up to us. Why? Because we imagine that being popular will make us happy. But happiness comes and goes throughout each day, like any fleeting emotion. Being popular can't sustain a state of happiness. No, what we are really looking for is to feel loved, and we imagine we will feel loved if we are popular. We may feel temporarily loved by those who jump on our bandwagon, only to jump off if we later prove ourselves unsatisfactory. In our minds, we know this desire to be a fool's errand. It has not escaped our notice that many of the world's most famously popular people suffer loneliness, addiction, and despair, sometimes even leading to suicide. What we really want is to feel loved even when we're *not* popular. We're looking for sustained love, unchanged by the world's shifting winds.

In my mid-thirties, I served as senior pastor of a five-hundred-member church in Washington State. It was my first senior pastorate, and I was very green. Looking back on that season of ministry, I remember how badly I wanted the congregation to like me. I was terrified to preach a sermon that might be received as anything less than a life-transforming home run. Making sure that everyone in the church was happy all the time, especially with me, was a driving force in my ministry. There were times when I mostly succeeded, and many more times when this goal was either impossible to reach or in conflict with the will of God as I saw it. Never did I find, in that congregation or any other, the infinite love for which I was still searching beneath everything else.

To name clearly what we are looking for helps us better to see where to find it. We are looking for that infinite love that alone can satisfy our souls. Our search for such love is first revealed when as children we experience the very finite love of our parents and caregivers. As our parents, who brought us into the world biologically, do their best to raise us, their finite love becomes a symbolic witness of the infinite love of God, who formed us in our mothers' wombs. When our parents fail to bear witness to God's infinite love and instead hurt or abuse us, or demand that we prove our worthiness to be loved, we become anxious and confused. Our trust gets shaken, and it becomes much harder to believe that there is an Eternal Lover who accepts and delights in us without limit or condition. It is when human love deeply disappoints us that we begin to strive to prove ourselves, anxiously searching for infinite love where it cannot be found— in external measures of worth by worldly standards like status, fame, or wealth. On the matter of our anxious search for love Henri writes:

> The human heart yearns for love: love without conditions, limitations, or restrictions. But no human being is

capable of offering such love, and each time we demand it we set ourselves on the road to violence.

How then can we live nonviolent lives? We must start by realizing that our restless hearts, yearning for perfect love, can only find that love through communion with the One who created them.[61]

Demanding unconditional love from one another without incorporating the boundless love of God is a recipe for bringing out violent behavior between us.

Jesus asks, "What are you looking for?" I've thought about this question a lot in my own life, and I know what a challenge it is to come up with an answer that is worthy of the question. If Jesus asked you this question face-to-face, how would you answer? In one sense, there are no "wrong" answers. On the surface we are looking for all kinds of things. Some of it is selfish; some of it comes from anxiety or pain: "I'm looking for a new relationship." "I'm looking for healing." Some of it is noble and caring: "I'm looking for world peace." "I'm looking for justice for the poor." "I'm looking for compassionate community." The way we respond reveals where we are in our life journeys and shows us what we most value.

Yet within and beyond even our highest desires, our souls ultimately crave infinite, unconditional love. Infinite love can be found only in an infinite heart, and only God has such a heart. The good news is that it is precisely this limitless love for which our souls are made. Henri, writing about the Eucharist, gives voice to this core of our faith:

> God created in our heart a yearning for communion that no one but God can, and wants, to fulfill. God knows

this. We seldom do. We keep looking somewhere else for that experience of belonging. We look at the splendor of nature, the excitement of history, and the attractiveness of people, but that simple breaking of the bread, so ordinary and unspectacular, seems such an unlikely place to find the communion for which we yearn.[62]

Yet even knowing this deep truth, Henri Nouwen continued to wrestle with Jesus' great question. "The world's love is and always will be conditional," he writes. "As long as I keep looking for my true self in the world of conditional love, I will remain 'hooked' to the world—trying, failing, and trying again. It is a world that fosters addictions because what it offers cannot satisfy the deepest craving of my heart."[63] Nouwen recognized that looking for fulfillment among the things of the world can only leave you empty, yet its appeal remains powerful.

Like us, the disciples in John's gospel may struggle with Jesus' pointed question yet intuitively sense what Jesus can offer them. We might picture them hesitating in the face of his question—letting their eyes drop, elbowing each other, scuffing their sandals on the pebbles. We might feel the unspoken tension in their minds: Is this a simple question, or something big we need to go deep with?

Finally, one replies in the form of another question: "Rabbi, where are you staying?" (John 1:38). At one level this is a literal, straightforward question, but in John's gospel questions and answers usually have more than one level of meaning. *The Orthodox Jewish Bible* translates the disciple's question: "Rebbe,...where is your dwelling place?" Where Jesus "dwells" may be interpreted as physical space or resonate with echoes of his interior dwelling in the Divine Life. These disciples, surely unaware that they are looking for infinite love, have nonetheless found him. They know at some level that they want to be with him where he "lives."

The grace of the story is found in Jesus' response. With his infinite love, Jesus simply says, "Come and see." Then he takes them to his dwelling place, and two more people find the fulfillment of their searching, at home with Jesus.

God invites us to bring all of our desires, shallow or deep, into our prayer and solitude. As we pray about these things, we eventually stop fretting so much over what we are looking for and start to pay more attention to the One with whom we are speaking. Then, we begin to realize that we too are at home with God, and prayer has fulfilled its purpose, drawing us into communion with the infinite love of God in Jesus Christ.

FRIENDSHIP

Friendship is one of the great expressions of human love. At its highest, it reflects the friendship Jesus extends to his disciples as they mature from "servants" of the Master to a deeper intimacy: "I do not call you servants any longer," Jesus tells them in his final earthly discourses, "but I have called you friends, because I have made known to you everything that I have heard from my Father" (John 15:15). This quality of friendship is rooted in the deepest form of love. Jesus is about to give up his life for the sake of the human race, and he has just commanded his disciples to "love one another as I have loved you." Only then does he say, "You are my friends if you do what I command you" (John 15:12–14). The mark of true friendship with Jesus is sharing in a love so complete it is willing to give its all for the well-being of the other. Few of us feel capable of this level of friendship, but we can all grow toward it.

As I reflect back over the many varied friendships I have had over the years and consider what the richest and most life-giving friendships have had in common, I would say they were all characterized by a high level of vulnerability. Vulnerability requires trust. As good friends share life experiences with one another over a period of time, trust grows. We begin to feel safe enough to share our deepest struggles and challenges with close friends. We learn to help one another, offering our time, our hands, and, most of all, our hearts. For me, the best friendships have grown organically over time.

I remember once as a teenager being part of a small group where vulnerability felt rather forced. We each went around the circle and confessed our sins, whether we wanted to or not. The group had certain consequences for sins like cheating, stealing, and lying. Usually, these consequences involved a few arm punches by the group members. It was meant to be semi-serious and semi-good fun, as teenage boys trying to follow Jesus and be tough at the same time.

Adults can have their own ways of punishing people for being vulnerable. But true friendships grow in richness, depth, and significance only when vulnerability is part of their natural rhythm. Not all friendships need to be deep in this way. Different relationships have different purposes. As we mature, we learn the importance of being discerning and careful about choosing those with whom it is safe and appropriate to be vulnerable, and to what degree. As a pastor, I am called to be an available safe place for parishioners to share their lives honestly and confess their sins vulnerably so that I may guide them in faith. In a similar way, each of us can offer safe space to our closest friends and family. We are all called to listen well to others, to offer our own life learnings, and to share God's healing, forgiving love.

All of us need friends with whom we can be vulnerable, no matter our age, gender, personality, or race; regardless of whether we are soft or tough, introverted or extroverted, gay or straight, hard-hat or artist. We have a profound human need for companions with whom to share our lives. Yet we live in a society now marked by deepening civil unrest and political animosity. People are at odds with each other over contentious issues. Friends have "unfriended" each other on social media over posts expressing personal opinions. We find ourselves caught up in what many have dubbed "the culture wars."

I wonder what Henri might say about this, if he were still with us. Would he say that precisely because of the prevalence of smartphones in our lives, we need incarnational spaces all the more—spaces where we look one another in the eyes, face to face; where we can hug, or shake hands? Recent coronavirus protocols have complicated this kind of personal connection while making more visible our need for it. Nouwen's timeless wisdom about the importance of vulnerability and safe space for one another certainly applies to our polarized culture. He lifts up for us the importance of nonjudging presence in our ministry of reconciliation:

> When we are free from the need to judge or condemn, we can become safe places for people to meet in vulnerability and take down the walls that separate them. Being deeply rooted in the love of God, we cannot help but invite people to love one another. When people realize that we have no hidden agendas or unspoken intentions, that we are not trying to gain any profit for ourselves, and that our only desire is for peace and reconciliation, they may then

find the inner freedom and courage to leave their guns at the door and enter into conversation with their enemies.

Many times this happens even without our planning. Our ministry of reconciliation most often takes place when we ourselves are least aware of it. Our simple, non-judgmental presence does it.[64]

This reconciling presence is a gift we as Christians can bring to the deep divisions of our day. Behind the antagonism of our "culture wars" lie a great many fears and anxieties. Fear is the great enemy of friendship and intimacy. Fear makes us run away from each other or cling to each other but does not create true intimacy. When Jesus was arrested in the Garden of Gethsemane, the disciples were overcome by fear, and they all "deserted him and ran away" (Matthew 26:56). Fear makes us move away from each other to a "safe distance," or move toward each other to a "safe closeness," but fear does not create the space where true intimacy can exist.

The tragedy is that we are often so possessed by fear that we do not trust our innermost self as a place of intimate divine encounter but anxiously wander around hoping to find it externally. Thus, we become strangers to ourselves, people who have an address but are never home and, hence, cannot be addressed by the true voice of love.

To those tormented by fear, who desperately look for the house of love where they can find the intimacy their hearts desire, Jesus says: "You have a home. Claim me as your home. You will find it to be the intimate place where I have found my own home. It is right where you are—in your innermost being, your heart." The more attentive we are to such words, the more we realize that we do not have to go far to find what we are searching for.

Nouwen would remind us that, above all, Jesus is our truest friend, our safe place—the One who says, "Come to me, all who labor and are heavy laden, and I will give you rest" (Matthew 11:28); the One who says, "I am the way, the truth, and the life" (John 14:6); the One who says, "Let not your hearts be troubled" (John 14:1). He will give us comfort, direction, and peace in his infinite love. From the experience of safety and peace in our own hearts, we find the freedom and courage to become true friends to others.

FORGIVENESS

It is impossible to talk about love without addressing forgiveness. Forgiveness is the great gift Jesus offers us on the cross, a cross that shows us the heart of God's love. When Jesus dies on that cross, darkness descends over the earth at midday. It is an image of the darkness of human sin, our state of alienation from God and from each other that makes forgiveness necessary.

Henri Nouwen knew the difference between living in such darkness and living in God's love:

> These dark powers have pervaded every part of our world to such a degree that we can never fully escape them. Still it is possible not to belong to these powers, not to build our dwelling place among them, but to choose the house of love as our home. This choice is made not just once and for all but by living a spiritual life, praying at all times and thus breathing God's breath.[65]

Author and pastor Richard Foster, in his book *Celebration of Discipline*, illustrates what this choice looks like. He writes about a time when he felt a need to come clean, to address unconfessed parts of his life that he sensed were blocking the flow of God's power in his life—preventing him from living in the house of love, if you will. So he divided his life into three periods: childhood, adolescence, and adulthood. Then he began by coming before God in prayer and meditation, with a pencil and paper, and asking God to reveal anything in his childhood that needed forgiveness or healing or both. He waited in silence and wrote everything down that came to his mind, with confidence that God would bring those things to light. The next day he did the same thing with his adolescence, and on the third day his adulthood. Then he took the paper to one of his closest friends and went through everything on the list, confessing all these unaddressed areas of his life. When Foster started to put the piece of paper back into his briefcase, his friend reached out and took it, tore the sheet into tiny pieces and dropped them in the wastebasket. Then his friend laid hands on him and prayed a prayer for healing for all the sorrows and hurts of the past.

Foster writes, "The power of that prayer lives with me today. I cannot say I experienced any dramatic feelings. I did not. In fact, the entire experience was an act of sheer obedience with no compelling feelings in the least. But I am convinced that it set me free in ways I had not known before. It seemed that I was released to explore what were for me new and uncharted regions of the Spirit."[66]

The forgiveness God promises us in Jesus Christ is meant to set us free, not only from the eternal consequences of sin, but also from its present power over our lives. Confession is the practice to which God responds with mercy and forgiveness. When we confess our faults, we bring them out from hiding and into the light of Jesus Christ. The Bible tells us, "If we confess our sins, he is faithful and just to forgive us our sins and to cleanse us from all unrighteousness" (1 John 1:9). As we are made clean through Christ, his brightness becomes our glory.

But sometimes our dark and secret habits can remain hidden for a long time, thus affecting other areas of our lives. Jesus puts it this way, "Your eye is the lamp of your body. If your eye is healthy, your whole body is full of light; but if it is not healthy, your body is full of darkness" (Luke 11:34). The darkness of sin can overshadow everything. Taking time to do self-examination with the help of a priest, pastor, or Christian friend can be one of the most spiritually healthy and liberating things we can do to dispel the darkness and come more fully into the light of Christ's love. Jesus continues, "If then your whole body is full of light, with no part of it in darkness, it will be as full of light as when a lamp gives you light with its rays" (Luke 11:36). Once we confess our darkness, we shine with blessings from above as God enters our hearts with forgiveness.

Confession is not telling God what he doesn't know. That's impossible. Confession is not complaining. If I merely recite my problems and rehash my woes, I'm whining. Confession is not blaming. Pointing fingers at others without pointing any at me feels good, but it doesn't promote healing. Confession is a radical reliance on grace. It is a proclamation of our trust in God's goodness. "What I did was harmful," we acknowledge, "but your grace is greater than my sin, so I confess it." If our understanding of grace is small, our confession will be small: reluctant, hesitant, hedged with excuses and qualifications. If we are full of fear of divine punishment, we won't have the courage to take a deep, close look at ourselves. But when we understand the boundless grace of Jesus Christ, an honest, cleansing, life-changing confession is possible, and we are set free from the chains of our past. Grace creates honest confession.

Nouwen writes about an openness that works hand in hand with forgiveness. "This openness, however, does not come simply of itself," he says. "It requires a confession that you are limited, dependent, weak and even sinful. Whenever you pray, you profess that you are not God nor do you want to be God, that you haven't reached your goal yet, that you never will reach it in this life, that you must constantly stretch out your hands and wait for the gift of life. This attitude is difficult because it makes you vulnerable."[67] There is vulnerability in the giving and receiving of forgiveness, and thus the giving and receiving of love. For we all are in need of forgiveness. Yet we are not always open to giving or receiving it.

In Matthew 18, Peter asks a question about how often he should forgive "my brother." In response Jesus tells a parable about a king who discovers that one of his servants owes him ten thousand talents. Now, a talent was a lot of money. It took the average worker fifteen years to earn the equivalent of one of them. In today's currency, ten thousand talents would be roughly 4–5 billion dollars, an astronomical and unrepayable sum for any servant.

Imagine that you are the man, and you are in a heap of trouble. How did you get in that kind of debt? Clearly, you are in way over your head, and now the note is due. Life as you have known it is over. Your wife, children, possessions—everything you have ever worked for—will be sold. And you're going to debtors' prison for a long, long time. You're ruined. People will only speak your name in sad whispers. So, you fall on your knees before the king and beg for patience, promising to repay it all. But both you and the king know this is impossible.

Fortunately for you, the king decides to forgive your debt and set you free. What a huge relief!

As the story goes, this servant who was forgiven so much went out from the king's presence (or we could say, he left church on Sunday after the Eucharist), and he found someone who owed him one hundred denarii. A denarius was a common laborer's daily wage, worth about twenty cents. The servant grabbed this man by the throat and demanded that he pay the twenty bucks. The poor man didn't have it and begged for mercy. But the servant wouldn't hear of it and threw this man into debtors' prison. When the king heard about this, he was so furious he threw the ungrateful servant into prison, where he remained.

Jesus looks at Peter and the other disciples and says, "So my heavenly Father will also do to every one of you if you do not forgive your brother or sister from your heart" (Matthew 18:35). His point is this: If you refuse to forgive another, that can only mean that you have refused to take to heart God's forgiveness of you, which can only mean that you are still imprisoned, unfree.

The problem is that we persist in defining ourselves by our hurts, our wounds, and our resentments. If we forgave, we would have to give up the hurt, without which we might not really know who we are anymore. If it wasn't for hurt and resentment, the daytime talk shows would go out of business. But the exhibitionism we see on television is only an extreme illustration of the more subtle tendency we all have to hold on to wounds at our core.

Have you ever noticed that when you are ready for someone to really know you, the time comes to tell that person about your deepest hurts? Somebody wronged you, you say. It may have been a parent, spouse, friend, or employer. Even as you tell the story, you can feel the pain as fresh as ever. The pain is usually accompanied by its twin, which is anger. And the anger digs at the hurt, refusing to allow it to heal.

When we tell these stories, we seem not to realize that our wounds are not really as attractive as we think. No one finds a gaping wound all that appealing. But scars—well, scars make a person rather interesting. Scars are wounds that no longer hurt because they've healed well. But they heal only because we have let go of our anger and resentment. And the only way to give up our anger at someone else is to forgive.

This is the point of Jesus' parable: remember how God has responded in mercy to the hurt you have caused him, and do likewise with your fellow human beings. We cannot call ourselves Christians—those who profess to live in Christ—and say that we do not know how to practice forgiveness. It may take some time for our wounds to heal. Forgiveness is often a process, not a single decision or proclamation. But at the least we need to seriously seek the healing of our wounds, so we can be released from their emotional hooks and freed to release others by the love of God.

Henri Nouwen speaks to the process of prayer that helps us move toward greater freedom, the freedom of the New Creation in Christ:

> The Christian...believes that God is not "something," but a person who is Love—perfect Love. The Christian knows it is possible to enter into dialogue with this loving God and so work at renewing the earth. Praying, therefore, is the most critical activity we are capable of, for when we pray, we are never satisfied with the world of here and now and are constantly striving to realize the new world, the first glimmers of which we have already seen.[68]

Forgiveness is part of perfect Love. It takes hurt out of the world, replacing it with love.

There are awful atrocities committed in our world, and millions who have suffered great injustices of hunger, poverty, violence, and racism. Yet many of us are awake nights fantasizing about how to get our hands around the throat of the person who owes us twenty bucks. Even if our hurts are more substantial, the question persists: "How long do you choose to be held in the past by the person who wounded you—the one who hurt you as a child, or took away your job, or walked out on you?" We certainly don't need to stay in relationships that abuse or harm us, but we can learn to forgive those who have harmed us. Forgiveness frees us from the prison of our own anger and resentment, which eats away our peace of heart and dilutes our creative energies.

How long do you want to be consumed with these personal debts while there is a world of grave injustice waiting for you to address it with the powerful, steadfast love of God? Only mercy can defeat hatred and hurt. The time to heal the woundedness is now. Nouwen urges us, "When you pray, you open yourself to the influence of the Power which has revealed itself as Love. That Power gives you freedom and independence. Once touched by this Power, you are no longer swayed back and forth by the countless opinions, ideas and feelings which flow through you. You have found a center for your life."[69] When God's love becomes the center of your life, forgiveness flows freely from you to others. And the forgiveness God grants to you in love unleashes new life and new love for yourself and those around you. Our only adequate response is to be grateful.

In Ephesians 4:32, the apostle Paul tells us that forgiving others is essentially a form of gratitude: "Be kind to one another, tenderhearted, forgiving one another as God in Christ Jesus has forgiven you." The great sin of our day is ingratitude. In our busy hustle to make sure we are receiving all that is coming to us, and in our compulsive need to keep our little justice ledgers, we rarely take time to stop and give thanks for the mercy of God. Can we really get off our knees after hearing, "In Jesus Christ we are forgiven," without being a changed man or woman? The biggest change is that we become grateful, and grateful people find that sharing God's mercy is not all that hard.

FROM LONELINESS TO BELONGING

Love gives us the gift of knowing that we belong to someone's heart. When we are loved, we feel valued, recognized, accepted, even cherished. Without relationships of love and friendship, we feel lonely. Signs of love take on new meaning when we are lonely. Henri Nouwen describes the experience this way: "The friend who cares makes it clear that whatever happens in the external world, being present to each other is what really matters. In fact, it matters more than pain, illness, or even death."[70]

Nouwen fought with feelings of loneliness throughout his life and came to this realization: "Most of my past life has been built around the idea that my value depends on what I do. I made it through grade school, high school, and university. I earned my degrees and awards and I made my career. Yes, with many others I fought my way up to the lonely top of a little success, a little popularity, and a little power."[71]

Notice how Henri identifies his focus on self and personal accomplishment as a source of his loneliness. When we work to distinguish ourselves from others, we tend to find ourselves separated from them. Humility is good medicine for this problem.

Yet Jesus was not focused on himself and still experienced feelings of loneliness. Anytime we are misunderstood by others, abandoned, or betrayed, we feel alone. Jesus was fully human, and loneliness is part of our human condition. During his forty-day wilderness sojourn, where no other person could have accompanied him, surely he felt intensely lonely at times. In the Garden of Gethsemane, the disciples whom Jesus loved and trusted the most, and who loved him the most, weren't there for him. He endured the greatest loneliness of all on the cross, where he felt abandoned even by God.

So, what did Jesus do with his loneliness? He didn't run away from it. He entered into it. Henri Nouwen saw this as the first stage in our own journey from loneliness to belonging. It's striking to me that we live in a world surrounded by people who are as lonely as we are, but rather than letting loneliness motivate us to reach out and connect with others, we soothe our felt emptiness with personal diversions or distractions. Nouwen believed that loneliness can be our motivation to move in three directions: inward, upward, and outward.

First, *inward*. Just as Jesus was not afraid to go all the way to the cross, so he invites us to go all the way in, to the cross of our loneliness. To feel it. To experience it. To suffer it. Rather than denying or avoiding loneliness, we must first accept it as the reality of our condition and situation. In our suffering we come to know something of Jesus' broken heart in its fruitfulness. As Nouwen prays,

> Thank you, Jesus, for the mystery of your broken heart, a heart broken by us and for us, that has become now the source of forgiveness and new life. The blood and water flowing from your side show me the new life that is given to me through your death. It is a life of intimate communion

with you and your Father. But it is also a life that calls me to give all that I am in the service of your love for the world.[72]

The experience of being alone causes us to use our own resources in new ways. Loneliness is an uncomfortable, barren landscape to walk through, as many have learned through the recent coronavirus epidemic. Help seems scarce. Oases are few and far between. We don't know when or if we will come out the other side. The familiar seems unfamiliar, and even well-known relationships can seem different in the midst of deep loneliness.

So the second step we must take is *upward*, to God. Only in God can we find the infinite love that forms the firm foundation of our lives so that we may flourish. Love grounds us in God and keeps us connected with each other. Jesus himself clarifies the order in his great commandment: "'You shall love the Lord your God with all your heart and with all your soul and with all your mind'...and... 'You shall love your neighbor as yourself'" (Matthew 22:37, 39). When we live inside love of God and love of neighbor, loneliness vanishes. In love, we discover that we belong to God and to one another.

This movement upward points to the difference between loneliness and solitude, a distinction that informed much of Nouwen's experience and writing. While loneliness can be destructive, solitude can be rich and rewarding, leading us deeper into loving union with God. Henri writes: "To claim the truth of ourselves we have to cling to our God in solitude as to the One who makes us who we are."[73] In Nouwen's view, we are called to be stewards of our solitude—to cultivate and protect it as an essential resource for life.

How can we sustain the gift of solitude when we feel a strong urge to be distracted by other people and activities? Like any spiritual discipline, it requires intention and commitment. We set aside time to read and ponder God's word, to pray and reflect, to journal with our insights. Simply by repeating quietly, "The Lord is my shepherd; I shall not want" (Psalm 23:1), or by meditating on an image of Jesus, we can lead our restless minds to a restful experience of the gentle Shepherd. We can begin to dwell at ease in the presence of Immanuel, "God with us."

Jesus gives us a beautiful image that can deepen the gift of our solitude and assuage our loneliness with assurance that we belong to his life in God. It is an image deeply familiar to the Jewish imagination: the grapevine. Like most of the Mediterranean area, ancient Israel depended on vineyards for livelihoods and sustenance. Vineyards were a central feature of both religion and culture; the prophets often referred to Israel herself as a vine. Jesus takes this central metaphor in a new direction. He identifies himself as the vine: "I am the vine, you are the branches," he says. "Abide in me as I abide in you" (John 15:4–5).

To "abide" means to dwell in, to live in, to make your home in. Nouwen describes the concept of abiding this way: "I deeply know that I have a home in Jesus, just as Jesus has a home in God. I know, too, that when I abide in Jesus I abide with him in God. 'Those who love me,' Jesus says, 'will be loved by my Father' (John 14:21). My true spiritual work is to let myself be loved, fully and completely, and to trust that in that love I will come to the fulfillment of my vocation. I keep trying to bring my wandering, restless, anxious self home, so that I can rest there in the embrace of love."[74]

In a physical grapevine, branches are connected to the vine, producing both vegetation and fruit. What does the branch do to produce fruit? Nothing, other than stay attached to the vine. The vine as a whole does all the work. The branch just needs to remain attached. In his metaphor, Jesus reminds us that we cannot bear fruit apart from him—apart from his life flowing in and through us, the way sap flows through the vine. In Christ, we know intimate communion with him who by his Spirit lives within us. His love is poured out as the essence of our very being, in which we find our source of life, joy, and belonging. At the same time, this "spiritual sap" allows us to "bear fruit"—to become fruitful in the world through our relationships with others.

Here we come to the final *outward* stage that Henri identifies in our movement from loneliness to belonging. In solitude, God prunes the unnecessary growth, those things in our life that diminish our fruitfulness in God's service. Solitude is a place of purifying our motives and clarifying our call in this world. The prophet Isaiah accused Israel of becoming a wild vine that had spent all its energy pursuing faithless paths, leaving it without fruit. Jesus presents himself as "the true vine" and his Father as "the vinegrower" (John 15:1). He is the fulfillment of Israel's covenant relationship with God, the one through whom genuine fruitfulness can be found.

As we abide in the true vine, we find that we are full of God's living energies—that our own well of love is being continually replenished and there is more than enough to share with others who are also in need. So the upward journey has led us outward. "This is my command," Jesus said: "love one another as I have loved you" (John 13:34). In that mutual love is the harmony of *shalom*, where we experience genuine belonging.

For Retreat and Reflection

QUESTIONS TO JOURNAL WITH *(select those that draw you)*

1. In what ways do you resist receiving love from others? When do you have difficulty offering love to others? Describe a time when you have known genuine mutuality in love. Note the gifts of this mutuality.

2. From whom have you sought acceptance, recognition, and affirmation? Identify a few places where you have looked for love and come away disappointed. What have you discovered about authentic love? Where have you received glimpses of God's infinite love?

3. With whom do you have the greatest freedom to share your vulnerabilities? Who feels safe enough with you to share their vulnerabilities? How do you cultivate a nonjudging presence that invites truth-telling? When have you witnessed or experienced genuine reconciliation in situations of conflict?

4. What do you need to be forgiven for? Whom do you need to forgive for being a limited and imperfect human being? What gift would forgiveness bring to you? What might it offer the offender?

5. What is your experience of loneliness? How is it qualitatively different from your experience of solitude with God? How do you cultivate the gift of solitude, and what are some of the fruits of your communion with the Trinity of love?

SPIRITUAL EXERCISES AND PRAYERFUL ACTIONS
A PRAYER OF IMAGINATION AND DIALOGUE

- Settle yourself quietly. Take a few deep breaths, breathing out slowly to release tension. Relax and open your heart.

- Imagine Jesus standing before you, looking at you with great tenderness and gentle seriousness. Hear him speak your name and ask: "What are you looking for?"

- Go into your heart to identify a strong desire or yearning. If it seems shallow, dig down a layer or two: What desire lies beneath the one you have recognized?

- Express to Jesus the deepest desire you are aware of.

- If it seems natural, imagine a dialogue with Jesus: speak with him and listen to him about what you are seeking. Capture the dialogue in your journal.

- Be sure to ask the risen Christ, through the Spirit, for the gift you most deeply desire. Express trust and gratitude that God will supply what is truly right and good for you.

AND/OR:

Write a brief confession and apology to someone you need forgiveness from. Write a letter of forgiveness to someone who needs to receive it from you. Pray about when/how to send these.

In the Next Chapter...

The love of God and the love it enables us to share with each other lie at the heart of all life. The great tapestry of divine love is a magnificent vision, a comforting promise of healing goodness and the fulfillment of our deepest human yearnings. It is tempting to see cosmic valentines and roses everywhere. But divine love is made of tougher stuff. Once again, we must recognize that love expressed in this world of brokenness, alienation, and conflict cannot escape the reality of suffering. Indeed, the most poignant and powerful expression of God's love for us comes in the form of an innocent man hanging on an instrument of brutal torture, entreating God's mercy toward a deeply unconscious humanity for their cruel injustice: "Father, forgive them; they know not what they do."

We have already commented on the connection between love and suffering. Henri Nouwen was fully aware of it, both theologically and in his lived experience. We know it in our lives too, although we struggle mightily to grasp why the sufferings we experience and see around us seem, at times, so permanently entrenched in this world. The pervasiveness of suffering baffles us, just as the origin of evil in God's good creation mystifies us. The two are linked but not identical. A great deal of human suffering is directly caused by selfishness, greed, and evil ideology. Yet untold suffering is also unleashed by natural forces we often call—for want of other explanation—"acts of God." Moreover, these forces wreak havoc not only on sinful humans but on innocent creatures.

It is time to explore more fully this realm we would rather not enter. How do we as Christians understand suffering? Does it hold a larger meaning and purpose for us? How do we endure, grow through, and offer up our suffering? How does our pain connect us with the life and death of Jesus, and how might his suffering transform ours? We are entering, metaphorically, the meaning of Holy Week.

CHAPTER FOUR

Suffering

Transforming Our Pain

Have you noticed how the frame we put around a painting can change how we see the picture? I once had a landscape painting with a heavy, dark frame. The art featured contrasts between deep shadows and bright areas of color. Not caring for the frame, I searched out a frame shop. In considering various samples, I discovered that colors in the frame made similar colors in the painting stand out. By selecting a light-colored frame, I saw light-struck areas of the picture I'd not noticed before.

Suffering is a universal human experience. It comes in ten thousand forms—physical, mental, emotional, and spiritual. The pain of suffering causes some to question the very existence of God and compels others to seek a closer relationship with our Divine Healer. Henri Nouwen understood that we have the power to choose how we will respond to the suffering that comes our way in life:

> We do have a choice, not so much in regard to the circumstances of our life, but in regard to the way we respond to these circumstances. Two people can be victims of the same accident. For the one, it becomes the source of resentment; for the other, the source of grat-

itude....Some people become bitter as they grow old. Others grow old joyfully. That does not mean that the life of those who become bitter was harder than the life of those who become joyful. It means that different choices were made, inner choices, choices of the heart.[75]

If we were to ask each of the accident victims why they feel resentment or gratitude, we would likely hear them describe their experiences quite differently. One might speak of the unfairness of the accident or of how his injuries deprive him of a normal life, feeding his jealousy of those who are unaccountably luckier. The other might describe how the difficulties of her injuries challenge her to find inner strength she didn't know she had, how her pain has opened her to compassion toward others who are hurting, or how grateful she is for the love and care of family, friends, and medical staff.

Each of us places some kind of frame around our personal experience of suffering. One frame may highlight the darkness of the picture, while another frame allows light and beauty to shine through. Nouwen tells us that we can choose a life-giving frame, and he calls this choice a form of "conversion."

Henri learned something about converting our perspectives by observing how Jesus responds to people's questions in the gospels. Jesus rarely answers a question on the same terms it is asked. The Pharisees bring him a woman caught in adultery and say, "The law of Moses says to stone her; what do you say?" Jesus turns their question back on them, replying in essence: "Which of you is sinless, that you may condemn the life of another sinner?" (John 8:1–11). His reply reveals that the question is rooted in limited human understanding. As Henri puts it:

Jesus answers from above to questions raised from below....He answers from a place far beyond the powers of the world. His answers come from his most intimate communion with God.[76]

The more we can choose a frame "from above" for our suffering, the more light we discover in our pain. The experiences of our lives, according to Nouwen, are a constant invitation to seek the meaning of our lives in God. Here is how he relates this to suffering:

The deep truth is that our human suffering need not be an obstacle to the joy and peace we so desire, but can become, instead, the means *to* it. The great secret of the spiritual life, the life of the Beloved Sons and Daughters of God, is that everything we live, be it gladness or sadness, joy or pain, health or illness, can all be part of the journey toward the full realization of our humanity.[77]

We taste how Henri invites us to convert our perspective as he describes one of his own most intense forms of suffering: loneliness. "The more I think about loneliness," he writes, "the more I think that the wound of loneliness is like the Grand Canyon—a deep incision in the surface of our existence which has become an inexhaustible source of beauty and self-understanding....The Christian way of life does not take away our loneliness; it protects and cherishes it as a precious gift."[78] The image of the Grand Canyon offers a new frame—one that invites us to see the immense depths within our solitary being, the beauty of interior vistas to explore, and the amazing possibilities of self-discovery. As we engage in this chapter the theme of suffering and how pain can be transformed, we will return frequently to the matter of how we frame our experience. The more we discover a God's-eye view "from above," the more meaning we find in both our joy and suffering.

BEFRIENDING OUR PAIN

> The first response, then, to our brokenness is to face it squarely and befriend it. This may seem quite unnatural. Our first, most spontaneous response to pain and suffering is to avoid it, to keep it at arm's length; to ignore, circumvent, or deny it. Suffering—be it physical, mental or emotional—is almost always experienced as an unwelcome intrusion into our lives, something that should not be there. It is difficult, if not impossible, to see anything positive in suffering; it must be avoided at all costs.
>
> When this is, indeed, our spontaneous attitude toward our brokenness, it is no surprise that befriending it seems, at first, masochistic. Still, my own pain in life has taught me that the first step to healing is not a step away from the pain, but a step toward it. When brokenness is, in fact, just as intimate a part of our being as... blessedness, we have to dare to overcome our fear and become familiar with it.[79]

Henri Nouwen is pointing here to one of the great paradoxes of human suffering. It is by entering our pain that we find our exit from it. Avoidance and denial only prolong the suffering, like untended wounds that fester. Suppressed pain spills out sideways in distorted ways. Accepting and entering our pain is the necessary first step toward its healing.

Of course, stepping toward and into our pain is never easy. Henri acknowledges this when he writes,

> You have been wounded in many ways. The more you open yourself to being healed, the more you will discover how deep your wounds are. You will be tempted to become discouraged, because under every wound you uncover you will find others. Your search for true healing will be a suffering search. Many tears still need to be shed.
>
> But do not be afraid. The simple fact that you are more aware of your wounds shows that you have sufficient strength to face them.[80]

It is natural to feel anxious as we face our inner landscape. Yet do not forget that Henri came to see the great wound of his loneliness as an abyss filled with inexhaustible beauty and self-discovery. There are profound and lovely gifts to be found in the depths of our being, because we are made in the image of God. However deeply buried or tarnished, the precious beauty of our soul is very much alive within the One "in whom we live and move and have our being" (Acts 17:28). But it takes courage to descend into the abyss, and we should not hesitate to ask for help in doing so. The Spirit places us in faithful community where we are called to "bear one another's burdens and so fulfill the law of Christ" (Galatians 6:2).

Nouwen encourages us not to be afraid, pointing out that greater awareness of our wounds is itself a sign of inner strength. Were we too weak to cope with our pains, we would not have the courage to recognize them. "The great challenge," Henri suggests, "is *living* your wounds through instead of *thinking* them through....The choice you face constantly is whether you are taking your hurts to your head or to your heart. In your head you can analyze them....But no final healing is likely to come from that source. You need to let your wounds go down into your heart. Then you can live them through and discover that they will not destroy you. Your heart is greater than your wounds."[81]

Here Henri gives us a new frame to place around our experience of pain. It has been said that the longest journey we will ever make is from the head to the heart. Rational analysis of our wounds can take us only so far. The heart takes us deeper. Our heart connects us to God through the heart of Christ, our healer. It is when we begin to live through our wounds in Christ that we come to know the transformation of pain.

Nouwen offers a beautiful picture of how we can comfort and calm our inner wounds, when he writes:

> Think of each wound as you would of a child who has been hurt by a friend. As long as that child is ranting and raving, trying to get back at the friend, one wound leads to another. But when the child can experience the consoling embrace of a parent, she or he can live through the pain, return to the friend, forgive, and build up a new relationship. Be gentle with yourself, and let your heart be your loving parent as you live your wounds through.[82]

We tend to think of our heart as the seat of human emotion, but the heart is a much larger reality than feelings alone. Ancient Jews and Christians saw the heart as the central organ of spiritual perception, including memory, imagination, and intuition. Thus the heart was the primary dimension of human life connecting us with God. This is why Henri can assure us that our hearts are greater than our wounds.

Henri's way of seeing each wound as a hurt child reminds me of the wisdom of another writer, Flora Wuellner. In several of her books on healing, Wuellner encourages us to picture each unhealed wound as an "inner child," hiding painful feelings under problematic behaviors. She reflects on the story of Jesus with blind Bartimaeus, who shouts after Jesus for mercy even when people try to silence him (see Mark 10:46–52). "Each of us has an inner Bartimaeus crying out," she writes, "often unheard or ignored by those around us and sometimes even by ourselves." Wuellner notes that "what we call our negative sides—anger, anxiety, complaining, criticizing, procrastinating, controlling, and so on—are usually deep inner cries for help." Perhaps they come from childhood traumas that we were told to get over, rise above, forgive and forget. "But wounds do not just go away," she continues. "If unhealed, they cry like abandoned children in the dark, forgotten places within us. The only way they can make their presence felt is through our negative attitudes, our addictive escapes, all symptoms of pain."[83]

Wuellner offers her readers guided meditations on inner healing. It may be useful to see how she guides such a meditation, to help us expand on Henri's image. This meditation emerges from Wuellner's reflection on the story of Jesus healing Bartimaeus. She sets it in the context of Jesus' question to the blind man—a question each of us may fruitfully ponder: Jesus stood still and said, "What do you want me to do for you?" (Mark 10:51).

- Make your body comfortable. Take a few slow, deep breaths; then breathe naturally.

- God's tenderness surrounds you. Rest in that deep strength. You are safely enfolded in loving attention. God hears your deepest needs, hurts, and longings. Breathe in God's love.

- Talk to God about some inner fault or compulsion that makes life harder for yourself and others; perhaps constant anxiety, excessive anger, overcontrol, jealousy, fear of intimacy, or an addictive habit.

- Picture God/Jesus lifting this inner "problem child," holding it close, listening to it, and laying hands of healing on it. Rest your body in this safe presence as God enfolds your inner problem with healing, transforming light. Take all the time you need.

- When you feel ready, stretch and gently massage your face and hands. Give thanks for any gifts received. Quietly leave your meditation, knowing that God's healing love still enfolds you.[84]

You might notice that Henri encourages each of us to act as a "parent" to comfort our wounded inner child, whereas Wuellner invites us to picture God as the one who holds and heals the wounded child within us. Each path is valid. Your own "good parenting" capacity is a reflection of the divine image in you—an expression of God's unconditional love and healing mercy. Since the love of God is already embedded deep in your soul by the grace of the Spirit, you can—in that same love—befriend and tend your own pain.

MOURNING OUR LOSSES

What to do with our losses?...We must mourn our losses. We cannot talk or act them away, but we can shed tears over them and allow ourselves to grieve deeply. To grieve is to allow our losses to tear apart feelings of security and safety and lead us to the painful truth of our brokenness. Our grief makes us experience the abyss of our own life in which nothing is settled, clear, or obvious, but everything is constantly shifting and changing....

But in the midst of all this pain, there is a...very surprising voice. It is the voice of the One who says: "Blessed are those who mourn: they shall be comforted." That's the unexpected news: there is a blessing hidden in our grief. Not those who comfort are blessed, but those who mourn! Somehow, in the midst of our tears, a gift is hidden. Somehow, in the midst of our mourning, the first steps of the dance take place. Somehow, the cries that well up from our losses belong to our songs of gratitude.[85]

Much suffering comes to us through circumstances beyond our control. Such losses are given, not chosen. The first task, says Henri, is to truly mourn our losses. We cannot evade the need to grieve. After my husband's unexpected death several years ago, I learned that grief has a life of its own. It is a process whose timing we do not control, and there are no shortcuts. Grief felt like an inescapable harrowing of my heart that left me totally spent. Yet Nouwen insists that we "allow our losses to tear apart" our sense of security in who we thought we were. It seems that unless life questions and shakes our identities, we see little reason to change, stretch, or find a larger identity in a greater Source.

It may seem the cup of suffering is thrust into our unwilling hands and we have no choice but to taste its bitterness. I had to swallow the sorrow of my loss, digest its pain, and absorb its reality before I could move into a new life without my beloved soulmate. From the abyss of pain and confusion, fear and fury, something new can—and does—arise. My personal experience with grief is but one example of what Henri means when he assures us "there is a blessing hidden in our grief" and a gift "in the midst of our tears."

In describing my grief as "the cup of suffering" I echo Jesus' prayer in Gethsemane: "Abba, Father, for you all things are possible; remove this cup from me" (Mark 14:36). We tend to assume that the wine in that cup is all suffering. Henri Nouwen, however, speaks of "drinking the cup" in a way that once again broadens our perspective.

For Henri, "the cup" is the *whole* of our life. He takes for his focus the story of the mother of James and John requesting of Jesus that her sons might sit at his right and left hand in his kingdom (see Matthew 20:20–23). Jesus replies directly to James and John, "You do not know what you are asking. Can you drink the cup that I am going to drink?" They reply, "We can." And Jesus responds, "Very well; you shall drink my cup," but goes on to say that seats in his kingdom can be given only by the Father's will. Nouwen, as a priest, was celebrating the Eucharist when Jesus' question, "Can you drink the cup?" pierced his heart. In his book by this title, he writes:

> It is the question that has the power to crack open a hard-ened heart and lay bare the tendons of the spiritual life.

"Can you drink the cup? Can you empty it to the dregs? Can you taste all the sorrows and joys? Can you live your life to the full whatever it will bring?"[86]

Nouwen draws three images from this question: holding our cup, lifting it up, and drinking it fully. Holding the cup means accepting our life as given: "What am I given to drink? What is in my cup?... We have to live our own life, not someone else's. We have to hold *our own* cup."[87]

There was a period of eleven years when my husband, John, and I had the care of both our mothers in our home. My mother was very fragile when she came to us, and her care brought me to a point of utter exhaustion by the time of her death twenty months later. John and I were just beginning to see light at the end of the tunnel when my mother-in-law, age 90, fell and broke her hip. I knew exactly what that meant—being thrust back into the intensity of elder care yet again. I did not want to hold my own cup!

"Drinking the cup of life makes our own everything we are living," says Henri. "It is saying, 'This is my life,' but also 'I want this to be my life.' Drinking the cup of life is fully appropriating and internalizing our own unique existence, with all its sorrows and joys." But I did not *want* the life I was facing after my mother-in-law broke her hip. Henri fully understood such resistance:

> For a long time we might not feel capable of accepting our own life; we might keep fighting for a better or at least a different life. Often a deep protest against our "fate" rises in us. We didn't choose our country, our parents, the color of our skin, our sexual orientation....

Sometimes we want to do every possible thing to change the circumstances of our life. We wish we were in another body, lived in another time, or had another mind! A cry can come out of our depths: "Why do I have to be this person? I didn't ask for it, and I don't want it."

But as we gradually come to befriend our own reality, to look with compassion at our own sorrows and joys, and as we are able to discover the unique potential of our way of being in the world, we can move beyond our protest, put the cup of our life to our lips and drink it, slowly, carefully, but fully.[88]

It took a while, but I did come to a more settled acceptance of the new reality of our lives as we cared for John's mother another nine years. Those years truly blended hardship and celebration. I learned to see her hidden gifts and the grace of mutuality in our relationship. I learned to accept and love her more fully. By the mercy of God, I was slowly able to hold, lift, and drink my own cup of life. In Henri's words, I was engaging in "the full celebration of being human."[89]

The Creator's beautiful plans will not be dimmed by human suffering. Even our most painful losses contribute to the threads God is weaving together into the magnificent tapestry that will reveal the completion of salvation: "We know that all things work together for good for those who love God" (Romans 8:28). Truly we can trust the plan set forth in Christ "for the fullness of time, to gather up all things in him, things in heaven and things on earth" (Ephesians 1:10). "All things on earth" certainly encompasses human suffering—a hope we can hold fast to.

CHOOSING JOY

One of the most radical demands for you and me is the discovery of our lives as a series of movements or passages. When we are born, we leave our mother's womb for the larger, brighter world of the family. It changes everything, and there is no going back. When we go to school, we leave our homes and families and move to a larger community of people....It all keeps changing. When we grow older, we retire or lose our jobs, and everything shifts again. It seems as though we are always passing from one phase to the next, gaining and losing someone, some place, something.

You live all these passages in an environment where you are constantly tempted to be destroyed by resentment, by anger, and by a feeling of being put down.... You find yourself disillusioned with the irrevocable personal losses: your health, your lover, your job, your hope, your dream. Your whole life is filled with losses, endless losses. And every time there are losses there are choices to be made. You choose to live your losses as passages to anger, blame, hatred, depression, and resentment, or you choose to let these losses be passages to something new, something wider, and deeper. The question is not how to avoid loss and make it not happen, but how to choose it as a passage, as an exodus to greater life and freedom.[90]

We have been introduced to the importance of choosing the frame we place around our experience, and the difference such frames can make to our perspective and attitudes. I had an opportunity to make such a choice at the moment of my husband's death. John died on our thirty-third wedding anniversary. I could see that as a painful double anniversary, or as a remarkable symbol of the gift of marriage given us to enjoy for thirty-three years to the day. I chose the latter. My frame looks like two bookends around our wedded life.

The way you choose to frame loss and pain shapes the lens of your perspective for other choices as well. When you choose a hopeful, life-affirming frame, it lays the groundwork for more positive attitudes as you face the future. If instead "you choose to live your losses as passages to anger, blame, hatred, depression, and resentment" as Henri put it, you effectively turn in on yourself and close off opportunities to see deeper meaning and find greater purpose in your suffering. Had I chosen to experience John's death on our anniversary as an entirely painful aligning of the stars, I would be focused each year on the unfairness of the timing; I would be trapped in the fruitless question, "Why?"

Our sufferings are surely the most challenging circumstances for choosing what can give us new life, larger perspectives, deeper connections with others and with our God. Henri encourages us to choose life—and with it to discover joy.

> For Jesus, joy is clearly a deeper and more truthful state of life than sorrow. He promises joy as the sign of new life: "You will be sorrowful, but your sorrow will turn to joy. A woman in childbirth suffers, because her time has come; but when she has given birth to the child she forgets the suffering in her joy that a human being has been born into the world. So it is with you: you are sad

now, but I shall see you again, and your hearts will be full of joy, and that joy no one shall take from you" (John 16:20b–22).[91]

Here Nouwen lifts up the process of moving from sorrow to joy, a sequence that gives us hope. The process was highlighted for me when, among all the sympathy cards I received after John's death, one stood out as a peculiar affront. It featured a bright sunflower on the cover and inside, the words: "Count it all joy" (James 1:2). This "condolence" felt like a stunningly insensitive message, completely ignoring my loss. How could I count as joy all that had just happened? I needed time to process the reality of sorrow. Eventually, I was able to glimpse the realm of joy Jesus was so deeply familiar with. The Spirit lifted my sight to a higher perspective where I could sense John's beautiful life held in the eternal embrace of God's love. His vitality was not lost but still available to me at a different level, penetrating my grief from a mysterious and wondrous dimension. This came as grace. Even if I cannot yet "count it all joy," I think I can "count it all grace"—and I suspect grace and joy are at least kissing cousins.

Henri continues his thoughts about Jesus' experience of joy:

Jesus connects joy with the promise of seeing him again. In this sense, it is similar to the joy we experience when a dear friend returns after a long absence. But Jesus makes it clear that joy is more than that. It is "his own joy," flowing from the love he shares with his heavenly Father and leading to completion. "Remain in my love...so that my own joy may be in you and your joy may be complete" (John 15:9b, and 11).[92]

Joy, Henri affirms, is intrinsically linked with love. His insight resonates deeply with me. After all, the experience of being loved certainly brings us joy; our acts of loving others also bring joy; even observing gestures of love shared between strangers elicits our joy. Love is the source of joy, as joy is an expression of love. If we know this truth from human experience, how much greater must be the knowing in Jesus' heart! The crucified Christ knows profoundly God's love for the whole world, and his Abba's love for him.

Such love carries us, too, into and through suffering. The more deeply we love, the more painful our loss of love. Love is the force behind empathy and compassion, enabling us to suffer with others. Love calls us to sacrifice our comfort, at times even to place ourselves at risk for the sake of others.

Since love is both the greatest source of joy and the strongest motive for engaging pain, we often experience suffering and joy together. They do not always follow stages—first the sorrow, then the joy. They can come intertwined as paradox: the "sweet sorrow" of pain in joy, and joy within suffering. Henri frequently addressed this paradox:

> Jesus calls us to recognize that gladness and sadness are never separate, that joy and sorrow really belong together, and that mourning and dancing are part of the same movement. That is why Jesus calls us to be grateful for every moment that we have lived and to claim our unique journey as God's way to mold our hearts to greater conformity with God's own.[93]

Because Jesus sees so clearly that "joy is a deeper and more truthful state than sorrow," we can have complete confidence that choosing joy is the most faithful path into the fullness of God's realm. On earth we rarely experience joy in its pure state, unmixed with disappointment, sadness, or longing for what we can't yet see. But Henri assures us that our lives, with all their challenges and triumphs, are the very ground from which God is forming us into the persons we are meant to become. God can use every part of our life experience to mold us more fully into the image of Christ, if we are open to being shaped. Choosing joy is a way of saying "Yes!" to that shaping hand. Through sorrow and joy together we come finally to the life that is all joy and light in the kingdom of grace.

SUFFERING IN CHRIST

"Can you drink the cup that I am going to drink?" Jesus asked his friends. They answered yes, but had no idea what he was talking about. Jesus' cup is the cup of sorrow, not just his own sorrow but the sorrow of the whole human race. It is a cup full of physical, mental, and spiritual anguish. It is the cup of starvation, torture, loneliness, rejection, abandonment....the cup full of bitterness. Who wants to drink it?[94]

The sufferings of this world are overwhelming—from the increasing intensity of natural disasters to addiction epidemics, from illnesses caused by toxic waste to the scourge of global pandemics and their trail of economic devastation. When we lift our eyes from the pains of our own small circles of acquaintance and survey the sorrows of those in other parts of our nation or world, it quickly becomes too much for us to comprehend and far too much to bear.

Even Jesus in Gethsemane, at the moment he faces directly into the agony to come, experiences anguish so deep that "his sweat fell to the ground like great drops of blood" (Luke 22:44). He prays earnestly for the cup to be removed from him. Nouwen imagines Jesus' state of mind in this moment: "Jesus couldn't face it. Too much pain to hold, too much suffering to embrace, too much agony to live through. He didn't feel he could drink that cup filled to the brim with sorrows."[95] Yet somehow Jesus finds the inner strength to complete his prayer with the words, "yet, not my will but yours be done" (Luke 22:42). Here Henri asks a very pointed question and offers a profound reply:

> Why then could he still say yes? I can't fully answer that question, except to say that beyond all the abandonment experienced in body and mind Jesus still had a spiritual bond with the one he called Abba. He possessed a trust beyond betrayal, a surrender beyond despair, a love beyond all fears....Notwithstanding his anguish, that bond of love had not been broken. It couldn't be felt in the body, nor thought through in the mind. But it was there...and it maintained the communion underneath all disruptions. It was that spiritual sinew...that made him hold on to the cup...willing to drink it to the dregs. This was not a show of willpower, staunch determination, or great heroism. This was a deep spiritual yes to Abba, the lover of his wounded heart.[96]

I have, perhaps, tasted something of what Nouwen is describing. After John's death, I experienced something new to me, and deeply distressing: a shattering of my trust in God. Literally hundreds of fervent, anguished prayers had been lifted for John's healing in that final month—my own and those of many friends, family members, and colleagues. It felt to me as if all of them had bounced off an invisible ceiling. Faith told me there was no one else to turn to but God, yet God seemed to have disappeared. I felt utterly trapped. I could feel nothing of divine love and sensed myself at the edge of an abyss: not only had I lost my husband, I seemed to have lost my relationship with God, compounding the anguish.

Then one day, while driving into town, I realized that somewhere deep down my trust in God was still intact. Relief flooded my heart. It was then I learned to distinguish between emotional trust and spiritual trust. Emotionally my trust was still shattered. But beneath the shards was solid ground—a deeper bedrock somehow undergirding my spirit, well below the surface of my feelings and conscious thoughts. Recognizing this mysterious reality was my personal awakening to what Henri calls "the spiritual sinew," an unbroken bond of connection with God. That realization marked a significant turning point in my recovery from grief. My relationship with God was broken only at the surface and could now be rebuilt on an even firmer foundation.

The cup of sorrow in human life feels ubiquitous and overwhelming. We cannot absorb its scope, and for all our efforts we cannot heal even a fraction of it. Yet all human suffering is connected because our lives are connected in God. As Henri reminds us, "For each of us our sorrows are deeply personal. For all of us our sorrows, too, are universal."[97] Jesus shares the deeply human struggle of accepting his personal suffering. Then he breaks open the larger, universal meaning God can give to our suffering. Like him, we can learn to connect with our spiritual sinew, entrusting both our life and our death to the One whose love for us is unbounded.

✳   ✳   ✳

When we say "Christ has died," we express the truth that
all human suffering in all times and places has been suffered by the Son of God who is also the Son of all humanity and thus has been lifted up into the inner life of
God. There is no suffering—no guilt, shame, loneliness,
hunger, oppression, or exploitation; no torture, impris-
onment, or murder; no violence or nuclear threat—that
has not been suffered by God.

There can be no human beings who are completely
alone in their sufferings since God, in and through Jesus,
has become Emmanuel, God with us.[98]

Jesus struggles to fully accept drinking the cup of his suffering. Yet
the depth of his anguish reveals that the struggle is not just about
his personal suffering. The cup before him in Gethsemane contains
the totality of human suffering through all the ages. So the greater
measure of the suffering Jesus submits to when he says "Yes" to his
Abba's will is not physical but spiritual. As God-with-us, Jesus can
bear the sufferings of humankind spiritually. Only in his divinity can
he transcend the limitations of his personal pain and open his heart
to absorb the brokenness and hostility of human alienation in all its
wretched forms. This is the full weight of Christ's reconciling work,
the purpose for which the Word became flesh. It is surely the dread-
ful weight of the world's pervasive sin and pain that Jesus hesitates to
take into himself, body and soul.

Nouwen develops his theme further:

We have to come to the inner knowledge that the agony of the world is God's agony. The agony of women, men, and children across the ages reveals to us the inexhaustible depth of God's agony that we glimpsed in the garden of Gethsemane. The deepest meaning of human history is the gradual unfolding of the suffering of Christ. As long as there is human history, the story of Christ's suffering has not yet been fully told.[99]

French philosopher Blaise Pascal (17th c.) once wrote that "Jesus will be in agony until the end of the world."[100] We may find perplexing the idea that Christ continues to suffer through our suffering. Yet the apostle Paul teaches that Christ suffers through his body on earth, the church. By taking up our own cross and following Jesus' example, we "fill up" or "complete" the sufferings of Christ (see Colossians 1:24). Jesus, by way of parable, also tells us that when we alleviate suffering for "the least of these," we are doing it for him, and when we do not, we are failing to recognize him in those who suffer (see Matthew 25:40, 45).

A great mystery of our faith is that we *participate* in the life of Christ and that he lives *in us* through the gift of the Spirit. We recognize and celebrate this spiritual union particularly in the sacraments of baptism and the Eucharist. Jesus uses the image of a vine with branches to describe our mutual indwelling, urging us as disciples to "Abide in me as I abide in you" (John 15:4). If we are joined to Christ who suffers with and for us, our own suffering is dignified with immense meaning. It becomes a way of participating in suffering that is redemptive. Suddenly our suffering has a profound purpose.

Henri discovered a remarkable trait among the handicapped members of the L'Arche Daybreak Community: "People asking not so much 'How can I get rid of my suffering?' but 'How can I make it an occasion for growth and insight?'...Among men and women rejected by a world that values only the whole and bright and healthy, I saw people learning how to make the connection between human suffering and God's suffering....They were asking how they could turn pain from a long interruption into an opportunity."[101]

Every form of distress in our lives—anxiety, exhaustion, illness, injustice, loss, or abuse—is an opportunity to give our pain to God. We can pray for our suffering to be made part of a redeeming purpose, as God works all things together for good. Mother Julian of Norwich writes of life: "It is a crucible for transformation. Each trial, every loss, is an opportunity for you to meet suffering with love and make of it an offering, a prayer."[102] Is this not precisely what Jesus does with his suffering? He meets it with love and makes of it an offering to God and a prayer of forgiveness. His suffering is transformed into infinite fruitfulness as the source of our redemption. Imagine our pain becoming part of that fruitfulness as we, too, choose to meet it with love and offer it up to God.

As Henri writes, "Suffering invites us to place our hurts in larger hands. In Christ we see God suffering—for us. And calling us to share in God's suffering love for a hurting world."[103] We can lift up our suffering to the One who takes it into his heart of infinite mercy, where forgiveness, healing, and new life become possible. As we join our suffering with that of Christ, God can bring from our pain the birth of a new creation.

DYING FRUITFULLY

One of the mysteries of life is that memory can often bring us closer to each other than can physical presence. Physical presence not only invites but also blocks intimate communication....

In absence, from a distance...we are less distracted by each other's idiosyncrasies and are better able to see and understand each other's inner core....

There is little doubt that memory can distort, falsify, and cause selective perception. But that is only one aspect....Memory also clarifies, purifies, brings into focus, and calls to the foreground hidden gifts. When a mother and father think of their children who have left home... when a husband and wife call each other to mind during long periods of absence, when friends recall their friends, it is often the very best that is evoked and the real beauty of the other that breaks through into consciousness.[104]

Henri Nouwen is articulating a tender and powerful truth about human life. The memory of one absent from us physically can illuminate that person's spirit with clarity. Nouwen illustrates this truth with ordinary relationships in daily life, yet the point he makes has special bearing on our experiences of death. In a sense, all human absences may be seen as dress rehearsals for the intensity of absence we feel in the face of death. The gift of memory can help sift gold from dross as we recall those we love who have died, and the potential of memory to evoke the best in others' lives can move us to ponder how our own death might be similarly fruitful.

Henri's insight is grounded in the life and teaching of Jesus:

> In his farewell discourse Jesus said to his disciples, "It
> is for your own good that I am going, because unless I
> go, the Advocate will not come to you; ...But when the
> Spirit of truth comes he will lead you to the complete
> truth" (John 16:7, 13). Here Jesus reveals to his closest
> friends that only in memory will real intimacy with him
> be possible, that only in memory will they experience the
> full meaning of what they have witnessed.[105]

In this passage, Jesus tells his disciples he still has many things to say
to them that would be too much for them to bear now. He will continue to teach them through the Spirit to come. Henri intuits that
our loved ones who pass beyond the boundary we call death may also
participate in how the Spirit guides us. In a book memorializing his
mother, he writes:

> To remember her...means making her a participant in
> God's ongoing work of redemption by allowing her to
> dispel in me a little more of my darkness and lead me
> a little closer to the light....In and through the Spirit of
> Christ, she indeed is becoming a part of my very being.[106]

Memory has power to help us distill the true essence of those who
have been most important to us. When such relationships have been
formed in Christ, their memory can gradually work to align us more
fully with the life of Christ. This insight offers a new frame for thinking about the legacy of memory and good influence we ourselves

hope to leave with others when we depart this world. Henri invites us to consider the quality of such "fruitfulness" in our death. It is not a morbid counsel but a call to choose deeper meaning and purpose in both our living and dying. Nouwen expanded his thoughts on this subject over time:

> Confronting death has helped me to understand...that I am called to die for others. The very simple truth is that the way in which I die affects many people....When I felt my death approaching, I suddenly realized how much I could influence the hearts of those whom I would leave behind. If I could truly say that I was grateful for what I had lived, eager to forgive and be forgiven, full of hope that those who loved me would continue their lives in joy and peace,...I would, in the hour of my death, reveal more true spiritual freedom than I had been able to reveal during all the years of my life. I realized on a very deep level that dying is the most important act of living.[107]

Henri wrote these words as he reflected on a near-death experience. He had been struck by a passing van while hurrying down a dark, icy thoroughfare in Toronto. Internal hemorrhaging almost took his life. From this close brush with death a rich mix of new experiences and spiritual insights emerged, one of which was the deep conviction that "dying in Christ can be, indeed, my greatest gift to others."[108] What did he mean?

Henri points out that Jesus' arc of ministry moves from the active to the passive. After three years of initiating ministry by teaching, preaching, and healing, Jesus enters into his passion. The words *pas-*

sive and *passion* are both rooted in the Latin *passio*, which means suffering or being acted upon. The fulfillment of Jesus' life purpose comes through giving himself up to those who resented and ridiculed him. "Jesus completed his mission on earth through being the passive subject of what others did to him."[109] Henri explores here another deep paradox: God's power is revealed in what we consider weakness.

We are taught to value success and productivity—through educational achievement, sports prowess, business profitability, political victory. We crave the signs of success offered in awards, diplomas, medals, trophies, and positions. But when our death is before us, we find ourselves weak and dependent. What lies beyond our success and productivity? Henri's answer: "*Fruitfulness* lies beyond and that fruitfulness comes through passion, or suffering. Just as the ground can only bear fruit if broken by the plow, our own lives can only be fruitful if opened through passion."[110]

This is how we participate in the mystery of the cross: "When Jesus was on the cross, his life became infinitely fruitful. There, the greatest weakness and the greatest strength met. We can participate in this mystery through our death."[111] To illustrate, Henri shares his thoughts on the dying months of his faithful office assistant, Connie. Connie was not afraid of death but worried for her adult children and grandchildren whose lives she could no longer be an active part of. Henri reflects:

> I wanted her to discover that the times when she needs them are as important as the times when they need her. In fact, in her illness, she has become their real teacher. She speaks to them about her gratitude for life, her trust in God, and her hope in a life beyond death. She shows

them real thankfulness for all the little things they do for her. She doesn't keep her tears or fears hidden...but she always returns to a smile....

Now, in her growing weakness, she who lived such a long and productive life gives what she couldn't give in her strength: a glimpse of the truth that love is stronger than death. Her grandchildren will reap the full fruits of that truth.[112]

Here, Nouwen introduces the idea that "in our dying we become parents of generations to come." He recalls many great saints and spiritual leaders who have left us a legacy of beauty and light. The lives and writings of these exemplars have become part of us, nurturing and guiding our own ideas and actions. This is what Henri means by fruitfulness. "Their joy, hope, courage, confidence, and trust haven't died with them but continue to blossom in our hearts....Indeed, these people keep sending the Spirit of Jesus to us and giving us the strength to be faithful in the journey we have begun."[113]

Life is full of openings to die little deaths: to choose the needs of others over our own desires, to choose service over power, humility over prestige, mercy over revenge. Each small dying to ego is a way of choosing Christ as Lord once again. Together our choices form new habits of heart, new patterns of intention that reshape us in the divine image. Countless little deaths prepare us for that moment when we are compelled to let go of all we have known—family, friends, earth's beauty, breath itself—allowing the homeward call of God to claim us wholly.

Nouwen's insight into the gift of our dying encompasses what we have explored in this chapter. The question of how to be fruitful beyond our years on earth shifts our attention from doing to being.

Being is a larger, brighter frame on life than doing. Like Jesus, Henri invites us to see our experience through a frame that lifts us to perceive "from above." His words stand as a fitting conclusion to the theme of suffering transformed into new life in Christ:

> Our doing brings success, but our being bears fruit. The great paradox of our lives is that we are often concerned about what we do...but we are most likely to be remembered for who we were. If the Spirit guides our lives—the Spirit of love, joy, peace, gentleness, forgiveness, courage, perseverance, hope, and faith—then that Spirit will not die but will continue to grow from generation to generation.[114]

For Retreat and Reflection

QUESTIONS TO JOURNAL WITH (select those that draw you)

1. What images or insights surface as you meditate with the phrase, "Let your heart be your loving parent as you live your wounds through"? How does the largeness of your heart connect with God's heart?

2. What parts of the "cup of your life" do you resist or wish you could change? How do you experience tears and laughter, grief and celebration, joined in your cup?

3. Identify a time when you experienced loss as a "passage" to something wider, deeper, or more life-giving. What was the role of your choice in this passage?

4. When have you experienced a shift of perspective on your pain that made it an occasion for growth? How can you choose to meet your suffering with love?

5. If you learned that you had one month more to live, what would become most important to you? What would you choose to do with your remaining days on earth?

SPIRITUAL EXERCISES AND PRAYER ACTIONS

- Identify one wounded child crying inside of you for healing. Using Flora Wuellner's meditation (p. 103) as a general guide, allow the Divine Healer to gently lift, tenderly hold, and lovingly attend to this hurt and anxious part of yourself.

AND/OR:

Reflect on how you would like to be remembered after your death. What qualities of your being do you hope to leave in the memory of family, friends, and coworkers? With this in mind, make a list of those you wish to express gratitude or love to and those with whom you need to seek forgiveness and reconciliation. Make a simple action plan to follow through on your intentions.

In the Next Chapter...

The theme of suffering is a difficult subject we often prefer to avoid looking at, even if we cannot escape its reality. As we have seen, however, it not only is impossible to sidestep in Christian theology by lies at the very heart of God's saving love for us. Sharing in the suffering love of Christ gives our own pain new meaning and purpose. And a significant aspect of that purpose has to do with our final theme, freedom.

In his letter to the Galatian church, St. Paul offers a memorable phrase: "For freedom Christ has set you free" (Galatians 5:1). Finding the view "from above" frees us from narrow vision. Discovering joy amid pain frees us from negativity. Forgiveness frees us from resentment. The whole program of Jesus' healing mission and redemptive work brings us to the great gift of spiritual freedom: freedom from illusion, freedom from the world's values, freedom from shame and guilt, freedom from judging others, freedom from destructive choices, freedom to love, even our enemies.

The gift of spiritual freedom leads us into the realm of joy and peace. Peace is a rare state of affairs in this world. Yet it is a central part of Jesus' mission and of our calling as ambassadors of reconciliation in his name. As we come to know the peace of Christ in our hearts and lives, we quite naturally become purveyors of peace in the world. The calm, clarity, and gentle humor of a peaceful soul quiets those around them.

But we live in highly anxious times that make finding such peace a real challenge. Henri gives us several lenses to look at how we can move from the ways of the world to the way of Jesus. Each one takes us deeper into the love of God, with more confident trust in the goodness that holds us eternally.

CHAPTER FIVE

Freedom

Finding Peace in Anxious Times

We live in an age of high anxiety. So rapid are the changes of this modern era that we struggle to cope with both its pace and scope. In a globalized world we are exposed to more information than we can absorb and more distressing news than we can process. The means of human destruction now include nuclear, biological, and technological warfare. Increasingly violent natural disasters assail us, along with the prospect of cataclysmic climate change. For good measure, add in a pandemic, economic crisis, food insecurity, social unrest, political divisiveness, and wars abroad. It seems the perfect storm for stress that can quickly become overwhelming.

Anxiety in the face of fearful forces is nothing new. Jesus understood well the nature of human worry. He addressed anxiety in his Sermon on the Mount, urging the ordinary people of his day: "Do not worry about your life, what you will eat or what you will drink, or about your body, what you will wear" (Matthew 6:25). Some of us don't worry much about such basic needs, but many in our world still do. Jesus might use different categories today, but his larger message would surely be consistent: Lift up your eyes to the Sustainer of all life in this world, from the smallest of creatures to the "crown of creation" in human beings. If God feeds the birds and clothes the lilies, why not trust the Creator to provide sustenance and protection for his most treasured creatures of all? The core of Jesus' teaching on anxiety is an invitation to trust God. He reorients us from the nose-length focus of worry to the availability, generosity, and good will of our heavenly Provider.

From childhood, Henri Nouwen was fascinated by trapeze artists. He drew several lessons from watching these remarkable acrobats of the air. A lesson from the "flyers" is the importance of letting go of the security of the bar in order to soar. Another lesson is the central role of the catcher. Far less glamorous, the catcher's role is nonetheless key to the beauty and wonder of a flyer's performance. Flyers cannot leap, twist, or flip without the steady, strong arms of the catcher ready at just the critical moment to catch them. Henri sees God as *our* catcher:

> Trust is the basis of life. Without trust, no human being can live. Trapeze artists offer a beautiful image of this. Flyers have to trust their catchers. They can do the most spectacular doubles, triples, or quadruples, but what finally makes their performance spectacular are the catchers who are there for them at the right time in the right place....Let's trust the Great Catcher.[115]

With God ready to meet our leaps, twists, and turns in life, we cannot be "dropped." Our divine Catcher is completely trustworthy. This gives us freedom to fly.

In an age of high anxiety we are deeply susceptible to the dynamics of fear and suspicion, anger and resentment, a grasping need for control, and an obsession with avoiding pain and death. These common responses to anxiety rob us of our spiritual birthright of inner freedom and peace. The image of God as a steady-handed catcher can offer us both comfort and courage as we let go of our own security bars and "fly" into an uncharted future. In this chapter, we explore several ways of learning to trust the Great Catcher as we move from anxiety to peace and reclaim the great gift of our freedom in Christ.

FROM FEAR TO LOVE

Many of us, if we are following Jesus at all, follow out of fear. But if we follow out of fear—fear of hell, of purgatory, of rejection, of not being acceptable—that is not following. Following Jesus cannot be a form of discipleship if it is out of fear. There is a lot of fear in us. Sometimes it overwhelms me how fearful we truly are….Jesus does not want us to follow him out of fear. He wants us to follow him out of love.[116]

As already pointed out, the opposite of love is not hate but fear. Fear is the source of hatred. The author of 1 John corroborates this point: "Perfect love casts out fear" (4:18). And along with fear, love surely casts out the negative emotions fear creates, including anger, envy, resentment, and hatred.

I would call our attention to two faces of fear: fear of God and fear of other people. Each is filled with distortion and healed only by love: love of God and love of neighbor. The cure for the twin faces of fear is precisely what Jesus identifies as the Great Commandment and its natural corollary: You shall love the Lord your God with all your heart and soul and mind; and love your neighbor as yourself (see Matthew 22:36–40).

In this chapter we will look at our fear of God. I do not mean fear in the sense of profound awe. When we read, "The fear of the Lord is the beginning of wisdom" (Psalm 111:10), *fear* has the connotation of reverential awe in light of the transcendent majesty and power of the Creator. Divine reality is far beyond our comprehension. Such wonder places us in a posture of natural humility and reverence.

No, by fear of God I mean craven terror—like standing before a judge we know will condemn and sentence us to death for our misdeeds. This is an entirely different posture—one we glimpse in the following Bible verse, which commends cringing servility to escape punishment:

> Serve the Lord with fear, with trembling kiss his feet, or
> he will be angry, and you will perish in the way; for his
> wrath is quickly kindled. PSALM 2:11-12

This Lord does not match the description God gives of himself to Moses on Mount Sinai: "The Lord, the Lord, the compassionate and gracious God, slow to anger, abounding in love and faithfulness" (Exodus 34:6). Indeed, the Lord of Psalm 2 sounds more like a cruel human potentate. Yet the Psalm 2 brand of fear has been fueled for hundreds of years by church teachings emphasizing the wrath of God and the hellfire of damnation. Generations of children have been deeply imprinted with guilt and shame as they imagined kneeling, or perhaps crumpling, at the feet of the Almighty.

Even after exposure to teaching on the love of God, many who grew up with images of divine wrath continue to harbor a deep fear of God. They cannot bring themselves to trust that God really accepts them, no matter how much they repent. I once knew a young woman who had worked herself into a state of emotional and spiritual terror. She was convinced she had committed "the unpardonable sin" against the Holy Spirit (Mark 3:29). While it seemed clear to me this was far from the case, nothing I said could convince her otherwise. Fear can keep believers in a state of childish passivity in relation to God—a state in which authentic spiritual growth is impossible. This kind of fear imprisons us in paralysis, depriving us of the interior freedom that is our spiritual birthright and that forms the ground of our maturation in Christ.

Even if we didn't grow up listening to sermons that frightened us with threats of a punishing God, or parents who tried to keep our behavior in line by assuring us that the heavenly Big Brother was watching our every move, we may still suffer pangs of anxiety about God. I have a wonderful picture of Jesus' face in my prayer room. The closer I draw to it, the more I see the immense, quiet love in his beautiful eyes. But when I stand at a distance, the face looks somber and stern to me. When I'm feeling guilty about my many failures in living faithfully or loving consistently, I tend to avoid looking at this face. My inner conflicts surface in a habit of distancing myself from the very presence that could heal me, if I would only draw near enough to see again the tenderness in those eyes. Guilty feelings bring to light my anxiety about God's judgment. This is only a milder form, along a spectrum, of our fear of God.

Any such fear, says Nouwen, is a world apart from what God wants for us. God *loves* us without limit and wants us to love him freely in response. "Don't be afraid," say the angels to Zechariah, to Mary at the Annunciation, to Joseph when he learns of Mary's pregnancy, to the women at Jesus' tomb after his resurrection. Do not fear the wonder of God, the visitation of angelic beings from a realm inspiring awe. God's messengers bring glad tidings of heaven's good will toward all humankind. God is communicating great love! Only a complete assurance of God's love for us can dissolve our fear of God. "Fear is not of God," writes Henri. "The love of God is the perfect love that breaks through the boundaries of our fear."[117]

Henri is uncompromising in his insistence that God's love is unconditional. Much of his own anguished spiritual journey revolved around hearing clearly what he calls "the inner voice of love." Here is one of his most powerful descriptions of the voice that transforms us:

> Do not run away from me. Come back to me—not once, not twice, but always again. You are my child. How can you ever doubt that I will embrace you again, hold you against my breast, kiss you and let my hands run through your hair? I am your God—the God of mercy and compassion, the God of pardon and love, the God of tenderness and care. Please do not say that I have given up on you...that there is no way back. It is not true. I so much want you to be with me....Do not judge yourself. Do not condemn yourself. Do not reject yourself. Let my love touch the deepest, most hidden corners of your heart and reveal to you your own beauty, a beauty that you have lost sight of, but which will become visible to you again in the light of my mercy.[118]

This, Henri assures, is the voice Jesus wants us to hear—the voice Jesus came to acquaint us with through his own life, death, and resurrection. The God revealed to us in Jesus is one who loves with generosity far beyond our deserving. We cannot earn such love; we can only receive it with gratitude and loving response. Fear is a prison from which God's love frees us. As Henri learned:

You will discover that the more love you take in and hold on to, the less fearful you will become. You will speak more simply, more directly, and more freely about what is important to you, without fear of other people's reactions.[119]

Along with Henri, we can learn to listen well and deeply to the liberating voice of Love. It is Love that catches us when we fall into destructive and self-defeating fear. We can trust the Great Catcher!

FROM RESENTMENT TO GRATITUDE

Resentment is cold anger....The greatest difficulty with resentment is that it's very hidden and interior as opposed to being overt. It has the potential to present itself as holiness and that makes it even more pernicious. Resentment resides in the very depths of our hearts... while we are mostly unaware of its presence. Whereas we might imagine that we are faithful and good, we may in fact be very lost in a much deeper way than someone who is overtly acting out.[120]

Henri Nouwen spent years reflecting on the parable we know as "The Prodigal Son" (Luke 15:11–32). Nouwen called this parable "The Story of Two Sons and Their Father." Jesus tells it as one of three parables in response to the Pharisees' and scribes' grumbling because Jesus "welcomed sinners and ate with them" (Luke 15:2). Each of the three parables points to how God searches and waits for those who are lost. The third and longest describes the father with his two sons. Here is my loose paraphrase of the story with a bit of commentary: The younger son asks for and takes his share of the father's inheritance before his father's death, a way of saying in effect, "I wish you were dead." He then goes abroad to waste his wealth on frivolous and riotous living. When he ends up destitute in a famine, he is reduced to feeding pigs. This defiles the young man in the eyes of his Jewish kin, who consider swine unclean. But since he is starving, the boy decides to return home where he knows that his father's servants at least get enough food. He doesn't expect to be welcomed as a son; he merely hopes his father will accept a well-rehearsed repentance speech and allow him to become one of the servants. But before he reaches home, his father is already out scanning the horizon. When he recognizes his son, the father is filled with compassion. This elderly family patriarch throws dignity and decorum to the wind and runs to receive his pig-filthy, exhausted boy with a wide embrace. So overjoyed is the father that he orders up a big party to celebrate— including a robe, sandals, and a ring, signifying the restoration of his son's status and dignity as an heir. Then the older brother comes home from the fields and hears music and dancing. Asking a servant what's going on, he learns of his younger brother's return and his father's joyful celebration. The older son is angry. When his father comes out to urge him to join the festivities, he lashes out in hurt: he has dutifully worked like a slave all these years for his father, who never gave him even a small party to celebrate with his friends, and now this younger son comes home after devouring his father's wealth with prostitutes, and he gets rewarded? The elder son is having no part of it. His father replies, "Son, you are always with me and everything I have is yours. It is only right to celebrate because this brother of yours was dead and has come to life; he was lost and is found" (Luke 15:31–32).

Henri saw his own life mirrored in each of the sons, and he eventually identified with the father as well. For those of us who may consider ourselves "good Christians," Nouwen's penetrating insight into the elder brother is perhaps the most revealing.

Nouwen was himself the eldest son in his family. He grew up absorbing many cultural and religious expectations to be an obedient and dutiful son who would not disappoint his parents or the moral authorities of his childhood. For this he was admired and respected. Yet being so "upright" came at the price of feeling burdened, even trapped. He watched his own younger siblings testing limits and living more freely. He couldn't help but notice that they were not reprimanded in the way he would have expected had *he* behaved in such ways. Henri describes watching his younger brother "fall apart" and confess everything to his father, while his father engaged in deep conversation and understanding with him. Henri saw a quality of intimacy between them that he deeply envied. Meanwhile he, the eldest, felt dependent on the constant need to work at being virtuous to earn not just respect but love and acceptance—a treasure that eluded him.

The elder son in the parable is furious at his father for welcoming home so easily the younger son who has wasted his portion of the father's inheritance and brought shame on the family through reprehensible behavior. Nouwen recognizes that the elder son, in his own way, is just as lost to his father as the younger one: "Outwardly, the elder son was faultless. But when confronted by his father's joy at the return of his younger brother, a dark power erupts in him and boils to the surface."[121] What erupts is resentment, envy, and bitter complaint. It is the resentment of the just and righteous, of those who work hard to be blameless. "There is so much judgment, condemnation, and prejudice among the 'saints,'" writes Henri, "so much frozen anger among the people who are so concerned about avoiding 'sin.'"[122] He sees in himself the "moralistic intensity" of self-righteous people, who regard themselves as superior yet feel they never receive their due for all the labor of being responsible, law-abiding people. Henri's inner "elder brother" left him less free and playful, and more envious of those who chose carefree and undisciplined lives.

Resentment is a common and pervasive weed in the garden of our heart. Its root goes deep and can be hard to pull out because it tangles around so many other roots. It is not just a weed but a poisonous one, damaging our relationships and corroding our capacity to love. Jealousy is a sister to resentment and equally toxic. Together they are powerful masters of emotion. We can lose our freedom in their tumultuous wake. But the Father's compassion is also available to us in our "elder brother" condition. We can still choose our response. However, this requires greater self-awareness. Henri models for us honest self-examination:

> Not having fully claimed myself as a beloved child of God...I divide my world between those on my side and those who are against me. In self-protection I cling to the few who respond to me, and I fearfully begin to challenge those who befriend my friends in case they steal affection away from me. I do this not because I am hateful, but because I am afraid and I view people with suspicion....When I sense danger, I become preoccupied with survival...and I withhold emotions, money, knowledge, material things, and love in case another will become stronger or more successful than me.[123]

We have looked at some ways we are fearful of God. Here, we turn to our fear of others. Henri sees clearly that when he does not claim his own belovedness, he becomes fearful of others as rivals to God's love and goodness.

The elder son in Jesus' parable also illustrates this fear. In his imagination, the father favors his younger son with undeserved love, rewarding bad behavior with a party. The elder son fears that his younger brother is usurping his father's love and attention. He thinks the father has never appreciated all his own hard work and obedience. In fact, he feels like a "slave," imprisoned in his role as the responsible son. He envies the joy his father takes in the younger son's return home. Comparing this to his own life, he feels deprived, left out. His father never gave even a small party to recognize or thank him for his loyalty and labor. (Notice how the elder son believes he should be able to *earn* his father's love.) Comparing his own worthiness with his younger brother's unworthiness, he feels self-righteous. His father's love for the younger is not only unfair; it is a threat to the privileged place he should have as the eldest.

Just as God's love is the only antidote to our fear of God, so it is the remedy for our fear of others. We need to accept deep in our being that God's love for us is unlimited and eternal and that this truth enfolds every other person as much as ourselves. We are completely precious in God's eyes, yet not specially favored because all are equally precious. "God shows no partiality" (Romans 2:11; Acts 10:34). Nouwen observes that the father in the parable, out of love, honors the journey of each son according to his uniqueness and weakness. To treat them the same way in the name of "fairness" would not be helpful. Henri observes, "I have to let go of all comparison, all rivalry and competition, and surrender to the Father's love. This requires a leap of faith because I have little experience of non-comparing love."[124]

In letting go of comparisons and accepting our belovedness, we are able to choose gratitude instead of resentment. According to Henri, gratitude is the opposite of resentment: "Resentment and gratitude cannot coexist, since resentment blocks the perception and experience of life as a gift. My resentment tells me that I don't receive what I deserve....Gratitude, however, goes beyond the 'mine' and 'thine' and claims the truth that all of life is a pure gift."[125]

Nouwen teaches that we can choose gratitude as a conscious practice. "I can choose to be grateful even when my emotions and feelings are still steeped in hurt and resentment....There is always the choice between resentment and gratitude because God has appeared in my darkness, urged me to come home, and declared in a voice filled with affection: 'You are with me always, and all I have is yours.'"[126] Henri encourages us to notice that with each choice of thankfulness, the next choice gets a bit easier and we begin to see more clearly how our ordinary lives are filled with grace.

Giving gratitude a chance to blossom in our lives often requires a leap of faith: "The leap of faith always means loving without expecting to be loved in return, giving without wanting to receive, inviting without hoping to be invited, holding without asking to be held."[127] This leap into the "thin air" of choosing thankfulness and graciousness in spite of hurt—not knowing what response we might receive, if any—is an act of trust.

In our many fears and jealousies, we are continually called to trust in the One who loves us without reserve, the One who runs to greet us every time we return home to the embrace of the divine heart. When we trust that immense, eternal love, we can feel gratitude and express love. Our leaps of faith are met with the strong arms of the Great Catcher.

FROM GRASPING TO FREEDOM

Praying is no easy matter. It demands a relationship in which you allow the other to enter into the very center of your person. The resistance to praying is like the resistance of tightly clenched fists. This image shows the tension, a desire to cling tightly to yourself, a greediness which betrays fear....The moment when you want to pray, everything returns: the bitterness, the hate, the jealousy, the disappointment, and the desire for revenge....You clutch them in your hands as if they were treasures you didn't want to let go...as if, in giving it up, you would lose your very self.[128]

Writing about the life of prayer, Henri Nouwen observes how tightly we grasp what we think gives us life. The image of clenched fists plays out in many ways. We clutch at security, control, status. We hold tightly to our sense of importance and belonging. We seek success and praise, imagining they can earn us love. We look for security in gated communities or by stashing emergency supplies in a bunker. We seek status in diplomas and titles or name-brand clothes and accessories. We shield ourselves from troubling questions by holding rigid ideologies and narrow beliefs. We wrap ourselves in a racial or ethnic identity to defend against differences. We grasp what we are afraid to lose. Anxiety constricts our freedom to live and love.

Henri identifies one of the most painful ways we hold clenched fists. Our inner world is often scarred by feelings of rejection, exclusion, and unworthiness in relation to the people or communities we most want to identify with. We crave acceptance among family and friends, in peer groups or circles of influence and expertise. All of us have felt wounded in relationships, and Henri points out that those we love most can most hurt us:

> Those who are closest to us are also those who cause us the deepest pain....Strangers and enemies are outsiders. We do not give them access to our innermost being. No, our real anguish comes from those who love us but who cannot love us in the way our heart desires. It is our father, our mother, our brother, our sister, our spouse, our closest friend, our co-worker, our neighbor who can hurt us most and be most hurt by us. It is with good reason that counselors and therapists always deal with these primary relationships. That is where we are most loved and most wounded. That is where our greatest joy and our greatest pain touch each other.[129]

This is the terrain Nouwen evokes when he says that in prayer, "Everything returns: the bitterness, hate, jealousy, disappointment, and desire for revenge." He knows what it is like to clutch these feelings as if they were treasures defining his very being. "I am struck by how I cling to my own wounded self," Henri writes. "Why do I think so much about the people who have offended or hurt me? Why do I allow them to have so much power over my feelings and emotions? It seems that in order to find my place in life I need to be angry, resentful, or hurt.... Part of me is 'the wounded one.' It is hard to know who I am when I can no longer point my finger at someone who is the cause of my pain!"[130]

A few years ago I recognized that I, too, held an identity as "the wounded one." My father was killed in a train accident when I was eight years old. My reaction to the sudden trauma of loss was to turn inward and protect my private grief. For years, I felt different from other children my age, few of whom had experienced such wrenching loss. I developed a strong inner identity as "the child who lost her father." It set me apart in my own mind and in many ways through my behavior. I was reserved, reticent, quiet. It took years for me to make good friends. With time, I grew out of my protective shell; yet only decades later have I understood how I created from that early wound an identity that defined and limited me.

Many things shape our sense of identity, any of which can become attachments we cling to in unhealthy ways. We get attached to material things that cannot satisfy our deep desires. We become attached to relationships that do not satisfy our emotional needs. Henri helps us see how we can also become attached to painful feelings that trap us in a false image of self.

In our search for authentic selfhood, we naturally want to be liked, praised, and accepted by others. What happens, then, to our sense of self when "important" people don't pay attention to us, or thank us, or recognize the value of our work? Does "selfhood" collapse? When Nouwen left the competitive world of academia and moved to the L'Arche Daybreak community, he learned a profound lesson in authentic selfhood. The core members of L'Arche communities are people with intellectual and physical disabilities. They knew and cared nothing about Henri's fame as a professor and author of worldwide renown. They simply recognized genuine love and responded to sincere care. Living in community with these remarkable people, Henri slowly learned to let go of his grasp on what he thought had given his life significance. He began to unclasp the tight fist of his attachment to praise and recognition. As he opened his hands to the L'Arche residents, he discovered a new freedom to be himself in more playful, humble ways.

Grasping what we think we need in life proves an unhelpful defense against our fears. The more we try to clutch possessions, plans, or people we want in our life, the more joy and freedom slip through our fingers. Efforts to make relationships meet our emotional needs push those nearest us away, creating only alienation. But God calls us to freedom. The Catcher invites the flyer to let go of the secure bar and brave the empty space that meets an open hand. "The great paradox is that in letting go, we receive."[131]

> There is a close connection between being called the beloved from all eternity and being free to love. Freedom is one of the essential qualities of the spiritual life. Love, communion, forgiveness—these all lead to freedom. Once we have claimed our true belonging, we are free to love.
>
> Being free to love is the most desirable freedom. It is the freedom to walk in this world without constantly being caught in the complex web of wounds and needs; it is the freedom to offer oneself without reserve. I know only a few people who have this freedom. But every time I meet people who are truly free to love, I feel drawn to them and want to be with them because of the space they create around themselves. It is a space in which growth is possible.[132]

Jesus calls the people around him to leave behind their ideas of security and follow him. The disciples leave their nets of secure employment, leave their families' emotional support, and open their lives to something new they can't yet know. It's a risk taken in faith. By worldly standards, life with Jesus is insecure and uncertain. Yet following him leads to the greatest gifts the human heart could ever seek: love and freedom. As Nouwen puts it, "Wherever we live, the invitation of Christ beckons us to move out of the house of fear into the house of love: to leave our possessiveness for a place of freedom."[133]

Paul's words in Galatians contain deep truth: "For freedom Christ has set us free" (5:1). We often think freedom means doing what we want when we want, like the prodigal son. But true freedom is spiritual, and its source is love. Freedom in Christ is the freedom to love as God loves. God's love far transcends our limited notions. Henri describes worldly love this way:

> The transactional quality of worldly love is precisely why people are always in trouble. If they give something they expect something in return. This is where the conflicts come from. This is where the hostility comes from. This is where the anger, jealousy, resentment, and revenge come from. This understanding of love is where the whole human chaos comes from.[134]

Jesus wants to free us from the chains of transactional love, which obligates us to return one good for another. The key to this freedom, according to Henri, is what he calls "the first love"—God's original blessing of love for us. It is given with no strings attached, no expectation of return, no obligations of duty. Love yearns to be responded to, but response has meaning only as a free offering. Love operates in freedom and creates freedom in our hearts to respond as we choose.

The woman who pours ointment on Jesus' feet and wipes them with her hair is expressing love and gratitude for being forgiven many sins (see Luke 7:36–48). Forgiveness expresses divine love. It is a free gift of mercy requiring no penalty to be paid and demanding no response. Receiving this gift has freed the woman from cultural norms in her day. She enters a gathering of men, most of whom disapprove of both her presence and her behavior toward Jesus. Yet she is free to offer her gift of love to him as an expression of gratitude and joy.

Henri sees that receiving God's "first love" frees us to forgive the wounds of our human condition. "Once we have heard the voice calling us the Beloved, and claimed the first unconditional love, we can see how we have demanded of people a love that only God can give. It is the knowledge of that first love that allows us to forgive those who have only a 'second' love to offer." Forgiveness is "the name of love practiced among people who love poorly."[135]

When we cling to our wounds as a source of identity, we resist healing. Closed and clutching hands cannot receive gifts. But when we accept that we have been God's Beloved ones long before anyone in this world wounded us and will remain Beloved long after we have left this world, we can begin to release our hands. Our true identity is eternally safe in God's love. We are freed from the need to wrest our worth from others. Finally, we can receive forgiveness and offer forgiveness from a place of interior freedom.

FROM ANXIETY TO PEACE

Our lives often seem like overpacked suitcases bursting at the seams. In fact, we are almost always aware of being behind schedule. There is a nagging sense that there are

unfinished tasks, unfulfilled promises, unrealized pro-
posals. There is always something else that we should
have remembered, done, or said.

In our production-oriented society, being busy,
having an occupation, has become one of the main ways
of identifying ourselves. More enslaving than our occupations, however, are our preoccupations. To be *pre*-
occupied means to fill our time and place long before we
are there. This is worrying in the more specific sense of
the word.

Much of our suffering is connected with these preoccupations. Possible career changes, possible family
conflicts, possible illnesses, possible disasters make us
anxious, fearful, suspicious, greedy, nervous, and morose.
They prevent us from feeling a real inner freedom.[136]

The values of our world conspire to keep us in a state of constant anxiety. Never-ending pressures to produce, succeed, excel, win, stand out
above the crowd, or even just keep our heads above water give daily
fodder for anxiety. There is so much to prove, so much to contend for,
so much to secure, protect, and defend.

Anxious thoughts tend to spin around our minds in a chaotic
jumble. Those who practice meditation call this "monkey mind"—
ideas and images jumping around like chimpanzees. Psychologists
call it "free association." We are all familiar with the experience: our
thoughts hop from a current circumstance to a memory to another
situation. Tracing back, we may see which association led to the next,
but the trail ends up far from where we started. Monkey mind tends
to get hooked by anxiety. Then thoughts begin circling obsessively

around our fears, pulling us deeper into them. Psychologists have a choice word for this: "catastrophizing." It can be difficult to pull ourselves out of the vortex when we're in the grip of such anxiety.

Jesus has a specific solution to the unhappiness of worry feeding itself. As already noted, Jesus gently chides us for being anxious about what to eat or wear and invites us to observe how God provides for even the humblest little creatures (Matthew 6:25–33). Then he goes further—right to the core. Here is how Henri describes it:

> Jesus does not respond to our worry-filled way of living by saying that we should not be so busy with worldly affairs....He asks us to shift the point of gravity, to relocate the center of our attention, to change our priorities....Jesus does not speak about a change of activities, a change in contacts, or even a change of pace. He speaks about a change of heart....This is the meaning of "Set your hearts on his kingdom first...and all these other things will be given you as well." What counts is where our hearts are. When we worry, we have our hearts in the wrong place. Jesus asks us to move our hearts to the center, where all other things fall into place.[137]

Shifting the center of gravity to a heart set on God makes all the difference. Nouwen links Jesus' words about the fruitlessness of anxiety with his response to Martha when she complains that Mary is not helping her with serving (see Luke 10:38–42). In that story, Jesus gently chides Martha for being "worried and distracted by many things" and urges her to recognize that "there is need of only one thing." The one thing necessary in both cases is to give one's heart to the holy Presence in the midst of all of life, to attend carefully to the voice from above, to set one's sights on the reign of God that Jesus calls "the kingdom."

Moving from anxiety to peace asks us to orient ourselves to the reality of the kingdom of God, a realm governed by a very different spirit from the one now governing this world. The Prince of this world directs attention to what looks successful, powerful, and impressive. The spirit of this world is unceasing competition, with winners and losers at every level—socially, economically, and politically. The world values pleasure, possessions, and prestige; it approves of amassing wealth and influence; it admires sports and entertainment stars. But none of these can bring us peace, personally or collectively. As Henri reminds us, "Somewhere deep in our hearts we already know that success, fame, influence, power, and money do not give us the inner joy and peace we crave."[138]

Nouwen speaks to the spirit of God's kingdom in contrast: "The Christian life calls for radical changes because the Christian assumes a critical distance from the world and, in spite of all contradictions, keeps saying that a new way of being human and a new way of peace are possible."[139]

Jesus calls us to live in the world from a different posture. His teachings make clear what this posture looks like in practical terms: The world tells us to hate our enemies, even to obliterate them; Jesus tells us to love our enemies and do good to those who hate us. The world tells us to take revenge when people wound or offend us; Jesus tells us to forgive "seventy times seven." The world tells us to get a return for what we give, plus interest. Jesus says to give without expecting a return. What accounts for this radically different posture? Henri says simply, "It is a life in which we are totally transformed by the Spirit of love....What is new is that we are set free from the compulsions of our world and have set our hearts on the only necessary thing."[140]

The apostle Paul writes, "Now instead of the spirit of the world, we have received the Spirit that comes from God, to teach us to understand the gifts that God has given us" (1 Corinthians 2:12). One of the greatest gifts of God is peace. In promising his disciples the gift of the Holy Spirit, Jesus says, "Peace I leave with you; my peace I give to you. I do not give to you as the world gives. Do not let your hearts be troubled, and do not let them be afraid" (John 14:27). The peace of Christ is the antithesis of the troubled heart and comes as a gift of the Holy Spirit.

To find such peace, the Spirit moves us along the same path of descent Jesus took. Not up the world's "ladder of success" that causes such anxiety, but downward into humility and simplicity, following the example of our Lord—the Mighty Word, who was from the beginning, emptied himself, and became one with a suffering humanity. Christ "moved from power to powerlessness, from greatness to smallness... from strength to weakness, from glory to ignominy."[141] The humble path downward to join the poor, the marginalized, the "least of these" is where we find peace. Why? Peace emerges from recognizing and celebrating our shared humanity, not from distinguishing and promoting our singular superiority. Peace blossoms where we discover unity and community rather than individual achievement and separateness.

Nouwen is clear that "the way of the Spirit differs radically from the way of the world."[142] The way of the world is rooted in anxiety that there isn't enough of what we need and that we ourselves aren't good enough. Our insecurity fuels competition for scarce goods, creating a fierce need for security, power, and control. This posture places self-preservation and self-promotion at the center, revealing a heart misdirected. Jesus, our Prince of Peace, says, "Set your heart first on the kingdom," and all these other needs will be met in relation to that new center of life (Matthew 6:33). He promises, "Take my yoke upon you, and learn from me; for I am gentle and humble in heart, and you will find rest for your souls" (Matthew 11:29). Entering into Jesus' spirit of humility and gentleness brings rest and peace to our world-weary souls.

When we are filled with peace in our hearts, it becomes possible to serve others as an effective peacemaker. We must know our inner warfare well, learn to observe our internal contradictions and struggles without condemning judgment, and accept and integrate our shadow side with humility and trust in God's grace. Then we can sit with those suffering interpersonal conflicts in a helpful way.

Nouwen recognizes a gift closely related to peace, especially when the peace within us finds expression in peacemaking. That gift is joy. We may know the quiet blending of peace and joy in our hearts, but Henri sees joy as the outward and visible sign of an authentic peacemaker:

> The "Yes" of the peacemaker is a joy-filled "Yes." The fruit of humility and compassion is joy. When we resist the powers of death and destruction with a sad heart we cannot bring peace. Joy is one of the most convincing signs that we work in the Spirit of Jesus. Jesus always promises joy; joy like the joy of a mother after childbirth (see John 16:21); a joy no one can take from us (see John 16:22); a joy not of this world but a participation in the divine joy; a joy that is complete (see John 15:11). There is probably no surer sign of a true peacemaker than joy.[143]

FROM LIFE TO DEATH

Somewhere deep in me, I sensed that my life was in real danger. And so I let myself enter into a place I had never been before: the portal of death. I wanted to "walk around" it, and make myself ready for a life beyond life.

What I experienced then was pure and unconditional love. Better still, an intensely personal presence...a very gentle, non-judgmental presence; a presence that simply asked me to trust and trust completely. All ambiguity and all uncertainty were gone. He was there, the Lord of my life, saying, "Come to me, come."

Death lost its power and shrank away in the Life and Love that surrounded me. All jealousies, resentments, and angers were being gently moved away, and I was being shown that Love and Life are greater, deeper, and stronger than any of the forces I had been worrying about.[144]

Just before a surgery that saved his life, Henri Nouwen entered into this profound spiritual experience. It was an assurance of divine presence and peace at a point of complete physical dependence on people and forces far beyond his control. Because he recovered, Henri had more time to reflect on the mysterious relationship between death and life. In a highly original insight, he saw that "claiming our second childhood" is part of preparing ourselves to die well. What is this "second childhood"?

Nouwen observes that early in life we rely on many people to help us survive and grow. As we get old and lose capability, we again need more people to help us survive. "Life is lived from dependence to dependence."[145] Jesus points in this direction when he tells his disciples, "Unless you change and become like children, you will never enter the kingdom of heaven" (Matthew 18:3). He is lifting up the humility and trust of a child as the path into God's realm. The second childhood Henri refers to is not, however, naive or immature like a young child. It is the humility and trust of those who know their dependency on God. In Romans 8, Paul writes: "When we cry, 'Abba! Father!' It is that very Spirit bearing witness with our spirit that we are children of God, and if children, then heirs, heirs of God and joint heirs with Christ—if in fact, we suffer with him so that we may also be glorified with him" (15–17). This, Nouwen says, "is the voice of a spiritually mature person...for whom complete dependence on God has become the source of strength, the basis of courage, and the secret of true inner freedom."[146]

From cradle to cross, Jesus models for us the movement from dependency to dependency. "Born in complete dependence on those who surrounded him, Jesus died as the passive victim of other people's actions and decisions. His was the journey from the first to the second childhood....He lived his life so that we may claim and reclaim our own childhood and thus make our death—as he did—into a new birth."[147]

The cross is a sign of the greatest paradox: death resides within our life, and life encircles our death. Henri puts it this way: "Death...is that moment in which total defeat and total victory are one....Jesus speaks about his death as being 'lifted up.' Lifted up on the cross as well as lifted up in the resurrection."[148] As with Jesus, our death is a passage into greater life.

Little more than a year ago, I sat beside my brother's deathbed and offered him the image of dying as a labor—the difficult, painful labor pangs that carry us through a passage into new birth. I used the analogy of a child in the womb, experiencing the pain and struggle of moving into this world—a realm as yet completely unknown to the child. I asked my brother, whose worldview was deeply shaped by science, if this image was helpful. He nodded. In the last weeks of his life, he had been sensing the presence of loved ones who long ago passed beyond the boundaries of this world. Death is a precious, holy threshold of passage, and it is a privilege to accompany others to its edge.

Watching with those who look death in the face gives us a glimpse into what Christ does for us in our journey from mortality into immortality. He is by our side in the transition, ready to relieve our anxious thoughts and bring us the peace of knowing that he himself is present in our life yet to come. Henri connects what he calls the sign of Jesus to the message of our eternal life with Christ:

> To look suffering and death straight in the face *and* to go
> through them oneself in the hope of a new God-given
> life: that is the sign of Jesus and of every human being
> who wishes to lead a spiritual life in imitation of him. It
> is the sign of the cross: the sign of suffering and death,
> but also of hope for total renewal.[149]

We know little of the realm of life beyond the one so familiar to us now. When we fear death, we struggle to hold on to what we know. But when we claim our place as God's children, heirs of the kingdom, we find freedom to release ourselves to this passage. Henri writes:

> When we can reach beyond our fears to the One who
> loves us with a love that was there before we were born
> and will be there after we die, even death will be unable

to take our freedom. Once we have come to the deep inner knowledge—a knowledge more of the heart than of the mind—that we are born out of love and will die into love, that this love is our true Father and Mother, then all forms of evil, illness, and death lose their final power over us.[150]

This freedom and confidence of the children of God is powerfully expressed by the apostle Paul in one of the most beautiful passages in Scripture: "For I am convinced that neither death, nor life, nor angels, nor rulers, nor things present, nor things to come, nor powers, nor height, nor depth, nor anything else in all creation will be able to separate us from the love of God in Christ Jesus our Lord" (Romans 8:38–39).

Nouwen tells us that the spiritual life is the life of God's Spirit in us. "God wants to be with us in a way that is so intimate and so personal that we can say God dwells in us. We breathe the Spirit of God. We start seeing what it means when Jesus finally says, 'I will be with you always until the end of time.' He means, 'I will be so intimately with you that you and I are one. You can breathe my breath and you can say, "Not I live anymore, but Christ lives in me."'"[151] With this profound communion in the Spirit, how could we ever imagine that our life is not safe in the Life of the One we are so deeply united with?

Late in his life, Henri had a chance to deepen his understanding of the dynamic between trapeze artists. He met Rodleigh, the leader of a performing troupe, who explained the real secret to Henri:

As a flyer, I must have complete trust in my catcher. The secret is that the flyer does nothing and the catcher does everything. When I fly to Joe, I have simply to stretch out my arms and hands and wait for him to catch me and pull me safely over the apron. The worst thing the flyer can do is to try to catch the catcher. If I grabbed Joe's wrists, I might break them, or he might break mine, and that would be the end for both of us. A flyer must fly, and a catcher must catch, and the flyer must trust, with outstretched arms, that his catcher will be there for him.[152]

Hearing this, Henri thought about Jesus' final words on the cross: "Father, into your hands I commend my spirit" (Luke 23:46). His reflections on this image will help us close this chapter:

Dying is trusting in the catcher. To care for the dying is to say, "Don't be afraid. Remember that you are the beloved child of God. He will be there when you make your long jump. Don't try to grab him; he will grab you. Just stretch out your arms and hands and trust, trust, trust."[153]

The same underlying message met Henri at "the portal of death"— where the Christ presence asked him to trust completely and "come home" to him. It is the presence that will meet us at the portal of our own death, ready to accompany us through the spiritual birth canal into life everlasting, where we will know beyond all shadow of doubt that Love is stronger than death.

For Retreat and Reflection

QUESTIONS TO JOURNAL WITH *(select those that draw you)*

1. What experiences have nurtured your confidence in God's love for you? What practices help you to hear "the inner voice of love"? How does its message free you?

2. How does playing the comparison game with others feed your resentment? When do you practice gratitude, and what feelings come into play when you dwell in it?

3. When have you left behind some form of security and discovered a new freedom you couldn't have known without the letting go? What hurts or fears have you held on to over time that have shaped your sense of identity? What freedom can you imagine flowing from their release?

4. What anxieties tend to preoccupy you? How do they affect your freedom and peace? When you allow yourself to follow the "downward pull" of humility and gentleness, how does it affect your inner freedom and peace?

5. What do you think mature dependence on God looks like? How might the image of dying as a passage through labor into a new spiritual birth help you prepare for your own death? How might it enable you more fruitfully to accompany others in dying?

SPIRITUAL EXERCISES AND PRAYERFUL ACTIONS

- Imagine yourself as a trapeze flyer, grasping the secure bar and preparing to leap. What is the "secure bar" you need to let go of to be free to fly in your life? Turn your gaze to the Great Catcher. Get in touch with the sense of complete security you have in those strong, trustworthy arms. Let that trust give you courage to let go of the security you've been trying to create for yourself.

AND/OR:

Read Genesis 2:7 and John 20:22.

Meditate on the image of God's breath in you.

If the Spirit of God is in you, and you are in Christ as he is in you, what assurance does this bring to your daily living?

How does this spiritual reality affect your contemplation of death?

Allow peace and gratitude to settle deep in your spirit.

Let adoration rise up in your heart, giving wings to your words and actions.

CHAPTER SIX

How, Then, Shall I Live?

Moving from Retreat to Call

We have been on a journey together—you, Henri Nouwen, and the authors of this book. We have moved from questions about human identity to the nature of God, in whose image we are made. We have explored the heart of divine love and grappled with the anguished mysteries of suffering. We have looked more closely at the gifts of freedom and peace on offer through life in Christ. Reflection questions, spiritual exercises, and action suggestions have helped us search our own minds and hearts in relation to these themes.

It is time to gather the fruits of retreat and ask: How is God calling me forward into newness of life? Where do I go with my fresh perspectives and insights? How shall I live my life in light of the journey I've just been through with Henri Nouwen's guidance?

Jesus assures us it is not those who say, "Lord, Lord," but those who do the will of the Father who truly belong to him (Matthew 7:21). How, then, will you act upon the word of grace you have received? This closing chapter presents you with an opportunity to integrate your learning through review, assessment, and discernment. Step out of the trees and see the woods. Listen to how the Spirit has been present through the whole process of reading, reflection, and meditation. Discern where you sense God's call as you move into new dimensions of your life.

This chapter is practical and interactive. You will need time to work through it, but there is no rush. It involves working extensively with your journal. Since it is useful to have everything related to this retreat collected in one place, I suggest you place these concluding reflections at the end of your journal. In the case of a physical notebook, you might use bookmarks or sticky tags to help you move back and forth between earlier and final portions of the journal. For online journaling, set up a temporary separate document so you can see both or toggle between them, adding the final portion into the larger document when complete.

REVIEW AND ASSESS

The first step is to review your journal notes. As you do so, pay attention to the questions you chose to respond to and those you did not. Which ones drew you, and why? Do you notice any pattern in the questions you gravitated toward? Take time to wonder about your choices, observing anything interesting or revealing in them. Sometimes the questions we choose *not* to dig into tell us as much about ourselves as the ones we do. That said, time constraints may have played a greater role in your choice than resistance. There is no need to judge yourself for any of the choices you made. The Spirit often signals to us through what we feel deeply drawn to. If, during review, you notice questions you didn't choose that you'd like to revisit with time, note them in this section of your journal. Apply the same review process to your spiritual exercises and prayerful action options.

Begin to assess your overall experience with this retreat. What has been *affirmed* that you already knew or believed? You brought lived and considered wisdom to this time; what has been deepened and expanded? What has *changed* in your way of seeing, understanding, or believing? As you read, prayed, and journaled, what shifted you to new ground? Do you see yourself, or God, in a new light? How do you think differently about love and suffering, or freedom and peace? Make note of learnings and perspectives gained. Which new perspective has been most life-giving for you? Are there ways your spiritual practice has already changed in the process of this retreat? If so, how? These are preliminary discernment questions. Now we will go deeper.

DISCERNING THE SPIRIT'S CALL

Henri Nouwen understood well the practice of discernment. He knew it as a gift rooted in prayer, attentive listening, and open-heartedness. "Finding ourselves in a relationship with God is prerequisite to discernment of God's will and direction," he writes. "Acceptance of God's will does not mean submission or resignation to 'whatever will be will be.' Rather, we actively wait for the Spirit to move and prompt, and then discern what we are to do next."[154] This progression mirrors what we are doing here. We have deepened our understanding of and relationship with God. Now we are actively seeking to discern "what we are to do next." Such discernment asks us to attend to the Spirit's movement in us.

Your journal can help you mine your experience of the Holy Spirit's presence through the retreat. Begin by taking each book chapter in turn. Scan the headings and recall basic points and stories. Think back to what spoke most deeply to you, whether in the book, your reflection on the questions, or your experience with the spiritual exercises. Where have you felt the Spirit of God at work in you? What does the Spirit bring back to your mind and heart that feels like a word spoken especially to you?

The Holy Spirit is persistent and doesn't mind repeating messages until we catch them. Did you hear a message repeated, perhaps in different chapters? Has a picture come to mind several times, perhaps in relation to different questions? Insights and images that recur are often clear signs of the Spirit's specific guidance.

Another indicator of the Spirit moving is through the energy we feel. Where have you experienced excitement, creative energy, or joy? Our God is a God of *life*, and life is always on the move, never static. Where have you felt drawn to newness, a sense of adventure, a desire to try something you have little experience with? St. Paul is offering spiritual realism when he says "If anyone is in Christ, there is a new creation" (1 Corinthians 5:17).

Creative energy and joy help us recognize where the Spirit is calling us. Nouwen writes, "The purpose of discernment is to know God's will, that is, to find, *accept*, and *affirm* the unique way in which God's love is manifest in our life."[155] What a freeing way to understand the divine will for us. It is suited exactly to who we are, to our unique being and gifts as expressions of God's love. Henri amplifies this insight: "Discernment helps us come to know our true identity in creation, vocation in the world, and unique place in history as an expression of divine love."[156] Just as Jesus came that we might have life in abundance (see John 10:10), we who follow his path are empowered by his Spirit to give life to others.

Because God creates us in love, and divine intention (will) for our lives is to express that love in our particular ways, a central question for discernment is: How have I been growing in love through this retreat? Where have I felt a shift in my heart toward greater love for God, for others, for my true self, for all of creation? How does this spirit of love want to move in me? Where does it yearn to take me? Is there a vocation I sense within the growth I am experiencing? The answer is likely to be found where you feel the strongest sense of connection with the material of this retreat.

When you have some clarity about the inner call rising out of your assessment and discernment, then ask: How do I carry the gift of this retreat into my life going forward? What container might hold the life-giving waters I have received as I journey on? How can I take the nourishment I've found and share it with others? This is where a simple rule of life can help us.

CREATING A SIMPLE RULE

A rule of life can be likened to a trellis supporting healthy plant growth. The trellis gives the plant enough space, air, and light to flourish freely. A rule of life is a pattern of practices that provide structure to strengthen a healthy spiritual life. These patterns help us create new habits of heart, mind, and hand, including attitudes and behaviors.

Any pattern of spiritual practice needs to be realistic. There is always a tension to navigate. You have awakened to a new desire, a sense of deeper call, a fresh direction in which the Spirit is drawing you. It is important to stay connected with your intention to mature spiritually through regular practice. You also need to balance this impetus with the realities of your life and personality. The mistake of the novice is to attempt too much in an over-eager enthusiasm for transformation. Slow and steady is the wisdom of our elders in matters of life-long practice. Learn to be faithful in small things, and God will know the time for more. In the spiritual life, small is beautiful, and perseverance is the key to growth.

Choose at least one practice that keeps you "rooted and grounded in love" (Ephesians 3:17). What will help you stay attuned to your desire to grow as you move into your new call? Perhaps five minutes of silence to absorb God's loving presence as you awaken, ending with a prayer for the Spirit to open your eyes to continued love as you move through daily tasks. Maybe ten minutes of reflection on a Scripture text using a devotional, while continuing your journal practice with a few jotted insights or wonderings. It could be a fifteen-minute walk, carrying a single-sentence prayer: "Lord, walk beside me and show me your way." "I lift my eyes to you, O God; reveal your light to me." Make the prayer your own.

In addition to a practice that strengthens your roots in God, choose one that orients you to the world. What might help you to further explore and express your emerging sense of vocation? This aspect of a rule of life can be quite practical. Here are a few elements of Martin Luther King Jr.'s rule for guiding the nonviolent civil rights movement: "Walk and talk in the manner of love, for God is love." "Observe with both friend and foe the ordinary rules of courtesy." "Refrain from violence of fist, tongue, or heart."[157] As you can see, such commitments can be deeply challenging aspects of a daily rule.

If you do no more than choose one practice in each category— nurturing both the vertical dimension of your life in Christ and the horizontal dimension of your life with others—and if your live into these relationships daily, you will further your vocation in this world immeasurably. Don't expect perfection! You will fall and fail regularly; we all do. But pick yourself up without beating yourself up and start again. Stay humble with the humble Christ. He is a gentle shepherd as we learn, with stumbling steps, to walk in the Spirit.

Henri Nouwen's deepest desire and call was to help root us in the love of Christ, where we discover our own eternal belovedness alongside the belovedness of all God has made. May that love fill and guide you as you learn to carry forward the gifts you have received in retreat with this wise teacher. Seek divine grace in your daily practice. Grace is the key to spiritual progress, the key to service in Christ's name, the key to Life itself!

ENDNOTES

INTRODUCTION

1   Henri J.M. Nouwen, *The Genesee Diary: Report from a Trappist Monastery* (Doubleday & Co., Inc., 1976), xii.

2   Ibid., 89.

3   Ibid., 103.

CHAPTER ONE: Identity

4   Henri J.M. Nouwen, *Out of Solitude: Three Meditations on the Christian Life* (Ave Maria Press, 1974), 34.

5   Henri J.M. Nouwen, *Life of the Beloved: Spiritual Living in a Secular World* (Crossroad, 1992), 28.

6   Ibid., 77.

7   Ibid., 57.

8   Ibid., 78.

9   Ibid., 31.

10   *Out of Solitude: Three Meditations on the Christian Life*, 22.

11   Henri J.M. Nouwen, *The Return of the Prodigal Son: A Story of Homecoming* (Image, 1994), 125.

12   Henri J.M. Nouwen, *The Inner Voice of Love: A Journey through Anguish to Freedom* (Doubleday, 1996), xiii.

13   Ibid., 70.

14   Ibid., 70.

15   Ibid., 67.

16   Ibid., 68.

17   Ibid., 8.

18   *Life of the Beloved*, 45.

19   Henri J.M. Nouwen, *The Way of the Heart: Connecting with God through Prayer, Wisdom, and Silence* (HarperCollins Publishers, 1981), 22–23.

20   Henri J.M. Nouwen, *The Road to Daybreak: A Spiritual Journey* (Image, 1988), 120–21.

21   Henri J.M. Nouwen, *Home Tonight: Further Reflections on the Parable of the Prodigal Son* (Image, 2009), 50.

22   *Life of the Beloved*, 49.

23   M. Craig Barnes, *Hustling God* (Zondervan, 2001), 20.

24   Ibid., 20.

25   *Home Tonight*, 50.

26   *Life of the Beloved*, 28.

27   Ibid., 27.

28   Henri J.M. Nouwen, complied and edited by Gabrielle Earnshaw, *You Are the Beloved: Daily Meditations for Spiritual Living* (Convergent Books, 2017), 4.

29   Henri J.M. Nouwen, *Intimacy* (HarperCollins Publishers, 1969), 15–16.

30   Henri J.M. Nouwen, *The Selfless Way of Christ: Downward Mobility and the Spiritual Life* (Orbis Books, 2007), 58.

CHAPTER TWO: God

31   Henri J.M. Nouwen, *Heart Speaks to Heart: Three Gospel Meditations on Jesus* (Ave Maria Press, 1989, 2007), 22.

32   Ibid., 22.

33   Henri J.M. Nouwen, *Compassion: A Reflection on the Christian Life* (Image, 1994), 18, 13, 15.

34   Henri J.M. Nouwen, *In the Name of Jesus: Reflections on Christian Leadership* (Crossroad, 1989), 25.

35   Henri J.M. Nouwen, *The Return of the Prodigal Son: A Story of Homecoming* (Image, 1994), 99.

36   Henri J.M. Nouwen, *Here and Now: Living in the Spirit* (Crossroad, 2006), 20.

37   Henri J.M. Nouwen, *The Road to Daybreak: A Spiritual Journey* (Image, 1990), 22.

38   *The Return of the Prodigal Son*, 96.

39   Ibid., 123.

40   *The Road to Daybreak*, 73–74.

41   *The Return of the Prodigal Son*, 100.

42   Henri J.M. Nouwen, *Lifesigns: Intimacy, Fecundity, and Ecstasy in Christian Perspective* (Image, 1986), 4.

43   Ibid., 9.

44   Ibid., 10.

45   Henri J.M. Nouwen, *Intimacy* (HarperCollins Publishers, 2009), 15–16.

46   Henri J.M. Nouwen, *With Open Hands* (Ave Maria Press, 2006), 21.

47   Blaise Pascal, *Pensées* (Penguin Books, 1995), 37.

48   Henri J.M. Nouwen, *Reaching Out: The Three Movements of the Spiritual Life* (Doubleday & Company Inc., 1975), 22–23.

49   Abba Moses, *Celtic Daily Prayer: Prayers and Readings from the Northumbria Community* (HarperCollins Publishers, 2002), 424.

50   *Reaching Out*, 106.

51   *Lifesigns*, 9–10.

52   Ibid., 3.

53   Henri J.M. Nouwen, *Turn My Mourning into Dancing: Finding Hope in Hard Times*, compiled and edited by Timothy Jones (Thomas Nelson, 2001), 34.

54   Henri J.M. Nouwen, *Bread for the Journey: A Daybook of Wisdom and Faith* (HarperCollins Publishers, 1997), February 29.

55   Henri J.M. Nouwen, *Clowning in Rome: Reflections on Solitutde, Celibacy, Prayer, and Contemplation* (Image, 1979), 13.

56   Kallistos Kataphygiotis (possibly 14th C, from *The Philokalia*), cited in Kallistos Ware, *The Orthodox Way* (St. Vladimir's Seminary Press, 1980), 32.

CHAPTER THREE: Love

57   Henri J.M. Nouwen, *The Inner Voice of Love: A Journey from Anguish to Freedom* (Doubleday, 1996), 59–60.

58   Ibid., 59.

59   Ibid., 59.

60   Henri J.M. Nouwen, *Here and Now: Living in the Spirit* (Crossroad, 1994), 103.

61   Henri J.M. Nouwen, *Bread for the Journey: A Daybook of Wisdom and Faith* (HarperCollins Publishers, 1997), January 20.

62   Henri J.M. Nouwen, *With Burning Hearts: A Meditation on the Eucharistic Life* (Orbis Books, 1994), 71.

63   Henri J.M. Nouwen, *The Return of the Prodigal Son: A Story of Homecoming* (Image, 1994), 42.

64   *Bread for the Journey*, December 28.

65   Henri J.M. Nouwen, *Behold the Beauty of the Lord: Praying with Icons* (Ave Maria Press, 1987), 19.

66   Richard Foster, *Celebration of Discipline: The Path to Spiritual Growth* (HarperCollins Publishers, 2018), 150.

67   Henri J.M. Nouwen, *With Open Hands* (Ave Maria Press, 1995), 44.

68   Ibid., 119.

69   Ibid., 120.

70 Henri J.M. Nouwen, *Out of Solitude: Three Meditations on the Christian Life* (Ave Maria Press, 1974), 35.

71 Henri J.M. Nouwen, *Finding My Way Home: Pathways to Life and the Spirit* (Crossroad, 2001), 64.

72 Henri J.M. Nouwen, *Heart Speaks to Heart: Three Gospel Meditations on Jesus* (Ave Maria Press, 1989), 43.

73 *Bread for the Journey*, August 16.

74 Henri J.M. Nouwen, *Sabbatical Journey: The Diary of His Final Year* (Crossroad, 1998), 165.

CHAPTER FOUR: Suffering

75 Henri J.M. Nouwen, *Here and Now: Living in the Spirit* (Crossroad, 1994), 27.

76 Ibid., 55.

77 Henri J.M. Nouwen, *Life of the Beloved: Spiritual Living in a Secular World* (Crossroad, 1992), 77.

78 Henri J.M. Nouwen, *The Wounded Healer* (Image, 1979), 84.

79 *Life of the Beloved*, 75–76.

80 Henri J.M. Nouwen, *The Inner Voice of Love: A Journey through Anguish to Freedom* (Doubleday, 1996), 109.

81 Ibid., 109–10.

82 Ibid., 110.

83 Flora Slosson Wuellner, *Miracle: When Christ Touches Our Deepest Need* (Upper Room Books, 2008), 25.

84 Abridged and adapted from *Miracle*, 29–30.

85 Henri J.M. Nouwen, *With Burning Hearts: A Meditation on the Eucharistic Life* (Orbis Books, 1994), 27–28.

86 Henri J.M. Nouwen, *Can You Drink the Cup?* (Ave Maria Press, 1996, 2006), 20.

87 Ibid., 27–28.

88 Ibid., 81–82.

89 Ibid., 21.

90 Henri J.M. Nouwen, *Finding My Way Home: Pathways to Life in the Spirit* (Crossroad, 2001), 135–37.

91 Henri J.M. Nouwen, *Lifesigns: Intimacy, Fecundity, and Ecstacy in Christian Perspective* (Doubleday, 1986), 87.

92 Ibid., 87.

93   Henri J.M. Nouwen, "All Is Grace," *Weavings* (November–December 1992): 40.

94   *Can You Drink the Cup?*, 35.

95   Ibid., 36.

96   Ibid., 36–37.

97   Ibid., 35.

98   Henri J.M. Nouwen, *The Road to Peace: Writings on Peace and Justice* (Orbis Books, 1998), 111.

99   Ibid., 112.

100 Blaise Pascal, *Pensees* (Penguin Books, 1966), 313.

101 Henri J.M. Nouwen, *Turn My Mourning into Dancing* (W Publishing Group, 2001), 6.

102 Mirabai Starr, *The Showings of Julian of Norwich: A New Translation* (Hampton Roads Publishing, 2013), xiv.

103 *Turn My Mourning into Dancing*, 11.

104 Henri J.M. Nouwen, *The Living Reminder: Service and Prayer in Memory of Jesus Christ* (Seabury Press, 1977), 39–41.

105 Ibid., 41.

106 Henri J.M. Nouwen, *In Memoriam* (Ave Maria Press, 1980), 60.

107 Henri J.M. Nouwen, *Beyond the Mirror: Reflections on Death and Life* (Crossroad, 1990), 51–52.

108 Ibid., 53.

109 Henri J.M. Nouwen, *Our Greatest Gift: A Meditation of Dying and Caring* (HarperCollins Publishers, 1994), 91.

110 Ibid., 92 (italics added).

111 Ibid., 94.

112 Ibid., 97.

113 Ibid., 98.

114 Ibid., 41–42.

CHAPTER FIVE: Freedom

115 Henri J.M. Nouwen, *Bread for the Journey: A Daybook of Wisdom and Faith* (HarperCollins, 1997), January 11.

116 Henri J.M. Nouwen, *Following Jesus: Finding Our Way Home in an Age of Anxiety*, ed. Gabrielle Earnshaw (Convergent, 2019), 86.

117 Ibid., 87.

118 Henri J.M. Nouwen, *The Road to Daybreak: A Spiritual Journey* (Doubleday, 1988), 157–58.

119 Henri J.M. Nouwen, *The Inner Voice of Love: A Journey through Anguish to Freedom* (Doubleday, 1996), 74.

120 Henri J.M. Nouwen, *Home Tonight: Further Reflections on the Parable of the Prodigal Son* (Doubleday, 2009), 60.

121 Henri J.M. Nouwen, *The Return of the Prodigal Son: A Story of Homecoming* (Continuum, 1992, 1995), 66.

122 Ibid., 67.

123 *Home Tonight*, 117.

124 *The Return of the Prodigal Son*, 76.

125 Ibid., 80.

126 Ibid., 80.

127 Ibid., 81.

128 Henri J.M. Nouwen, *With Open Hands* (Ave Maria Press, 1995), 11–12, 14.

129 Henri J.M. Nouwen, "Forgiveness: The Name of Love in a Wounded World" (*Weavings*, Vol. 7, No. 2), 13.

130 Ibid., 14.

131 Henri J.M. Nouwen, *Turn My Mourning into Dancing* (W Publishing Group, 2001), 26.

132 "Forgiveness: The Name of Love in a Wounded World," 15.

133 *Turn My Mourning into Dancing*, 33.

134 *Following Jesus*, 58.

135 "Forgiveness: The Name of Love in a Wounded World," 14–15, abridged.

136 Henri J.M. Nouwen, *Making All Things New: An Invitation to the Spiritual Life* (Harper & Row, 1981), abridged from selected portions, 23–27.

137 Ibid., 41–43.

138 Henri J.M. Nouwen, *The Selfless Way of Christ: Downward Mobility and the Spiritual Life* (Orbis Books, 2007), 34.

139 *With Open Hands*, 105.

140 *Making All Things New*, 56–57.

141 *The Selfless Way of Christ*, 31.

142 Ibid, 39.

143 Henri J.M. Nouwen, *The Road to Peace* (Orbis Books, 1998), 47.

144   Henri J.M. Nouwen, *Beyond the Mirror: Reflections on Death and Life* (Crossroad, 1990), 34–37, abridged.

145   Henri J.M. Nouwen, *Our Greatest Gift: A Meditation of Dying and Caring* (HarperCollins Publishers, 1994), 14.

146   Ibid., 19.

147   Ibid., 14–15.

148   Henri J.M. Nouwen, *Here and Now: Living in the Spirit* (Crossroad, 1994), 139–40.

149   Henri J.M. Nouwen, *Letters to Marc about Jesus* (Harper & Row, 1988), 30.

150   *Our Greatest Gift*, 17, abridged.

151   *Following Jesus*, 115–16, abridged.

152   *Our Greatest Gift*, 66–67, abridged.

153   Ibid., 67.

CHAPTER SIX: How, Then, Shall I Live?

154   Henri J.M. Nouwen, with Michael J. Christensen & Rebecca J. Laird, *Discernment: Reading the Signs of Daily Life* (HarperOne, 2013 by the estate of Henri J.M. Nouwen), 8.

155   Ibid.

156   Ibid, 6.

157   As adapted by William O. Paulsell from Martin Luther King Jr., *Why We Can't Wait* (Signet Books, 1964), 69.